Math for College and Career Readiness
Grade 7

Authors: Christine Henderson (Ed.), Karise Mace, Stephen Fowler, Amy Jones-Lewis

Editor: Mary Dieterich

Proofreaders: April Albert and Margaret Brown

COPYRIGHT © 2016 Mark Twain Media, Inc.

ISBN 978-1-62223-584-1

Printing No. CD-404239

Mark Twain Media, Inc., Publishers
Distributed by Carson-Dellosa Publishing LLC

Table of Contents

Introduction to the Teacher

Up to half of students entering college elect "undecided" for their major, and an estimated three out of four students change their majors at least once before graduation. This is, in part, due to the fact that middle- and high-school students do not have much exposure to the variety of careers available to today's work force. This workbook is designed to give middle-school students an idea of existing careers and the background and skills necessary to be successful in those careers.

The first three units focus on jobs students could do right now to start building their resumes and earning some money. The next three units focus on careers that require at least some post-secondary schooling. The final three units emphasize STEM-related careers, where science, technology, engineering, and mathematics play a significant part.

Each unit is aligned to the Common Core State Standards for Mathematics. This correlation is included on the teacher page at the beginning of each unit. The units also support the NCTM standards. The teacher page also includes background on the career, the average median salary listed by the 2015 U.S. Bureau of Labor Statistics, a detailed explanation of the topics covered in the unit, and a list of prerequisite skills necessary to complete the unit.

We hope your students enjoy exploring these different careers and that this exploration helps prepare them for college and their future careers.

—Stephen Fowler, Christine Henderson, Amy Jones-Lewis, and Karise Mace

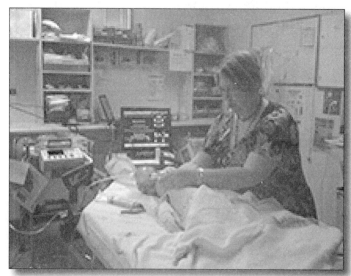

Unit 1: The Mathematics of Lawn Care

Introduction

There is always work to be done in the yard! This is particularly true in parts of the country that experience four seasons throughout the year. Anyone willing to work hard could make a lot of money by offering his or her services—cutting grass in the summer, raking leaves in the fall, shoveling snow in the winter, and planting flowers in the spring.

While this may sound like it is all physical labor, there is quite a bit of mathematics involved. Besides calculating how much to charge for the time it takes to do the work, a good entrepreneur is also taking into account the expenses that s/he will incur. In many cases, the area of land to be cared for must be accounted for to correctly estimate costs and charges. The entrepreneur also has to consider how to map out his/her travel through the neighborhood to make sure that time isn't wasted.

If someone is interested in providing these services but does not think through all of the details, s/he is at risk of losing money on a lot of manual labor.

These are just some of the ways mathematics is used to run a business and will be the focus of this unit as students explore the math needed to run a lawn care business.

Common Core State Standards

This unit addresses the following Common Core State Standards:

- CCSS.Math.Content.7.EE.B.4B
- CCSS.Math.Content.7.NS.A.2C
- CCSS.Math.Content.7.NS.A.3
- CCSS.Math.Content.7.G.B6

Prerequisite Skills

Prior to completing this unit, students should be proficient in the following mathematical skills: (Note: A practice sheet has been provided for each skill listed.)

- Solving two-step inequalities
- Subtracting integers
- Calculating area of composite figures

Name: _____ Date: _____

Unit 1: The Mathematics of Lawn Care

Prerequisite Skill Practice—Two-Step Inequalities

Directions: Solve each inequality. Show your work. The first problem has been worked out as an example.

1. $8 > -4x - 2$ $$8 > -4x - 2$$ $$8 + 2 > -4x - 2 + 2$$ $$10 > -4x$$ $$\frac{10}{-4} < \frac{-4x}{-4}$$ $$-2\frac{1}{2} < x$$	**2.** $5 \leq 11 + 3x$
3. $2x - 7 < -5$	**4.** $-18 \leq -7x - 4$
5. $-5x + 1 < 1$	**6.** $-15 \geq 4x + 3$
7. $-7 \geq -3 + \frac{1}{5}x$	**8.** $-2 - \frac{2}{3}x \geq 6$

Name: _____ Date: _____

Unit 1: The Mathematics of Lawn Care

Prerequisite Skill Practice—Integer Subtraction

Directions: Subtract. Show your work. The first problem has been worked out as an example.

1. 14 − 17 14 − 17 14 + (−17) −|17 − 14| −3	**2.** −10 − 19
3. −23 − (−15)	**4.** 34 − 90
5. −28 − 34	**6.** 44 − (−7)
7. 12 − 59	**8.** −17 − (−52)

Name: _____   Date: _____

Unit 1: The Mathematics of Lawn Care

Prerequisite Skill Practice—Area of Composite Figures

Directions: Determine the area of the following shapes and show your work. The first problem has been worked out as an example. Use 3.1415 as π.

1.

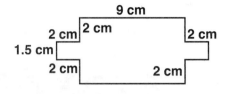

9(2 + 2 + 1.5) + 2(2(1.5))
9(5.5) + 2(3)
49.5 + 6
55.5
The area is 55.5 square centimeters.

2.

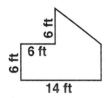

3.

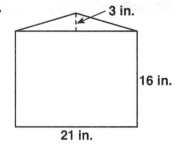

4.

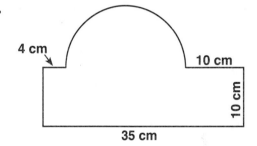

5.

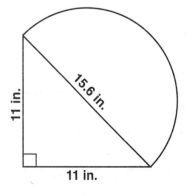

6.

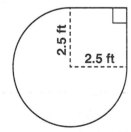

Name: _____ Date: _____

Unit 1: The Mathematics of Lawn Care

Real-Life Application

Mowing Lawns

Oscar is mowing lawns to earn money for a new trumpet that costs $450.

1. Before he can start mowing, he has to buy the necessary tools: a lawnmower, a weed trimmer, fertilizer, and a gas can.

Item	Quantity	Price per unit
Lawnmower	1	$179.95
Weed trimmer	1	$89.95
Fertilizer	5	$24.97
Gas can	1	$20.95

What is the total cost of these expenses? Show your work.

_____

2. On average, Oscar charges $35 for each lawn he mows. Given his expenses, how many lawns does he need to mow to earn at least $450 for the new trumpet? Write and solve an inequality to answer the question.

_____

_____

3. For his birthday, Oscar's mom gives him a $200 gift card. If he uses that to help pay for the lawn-care tools, how many lawns does Oscar need to mow to afford his new trumpet? Write and solve an inequality to answer the question.

_____

_____

Name: _____ Date: _____

Unit 1: The Mathematics of Lawn Care

Real-Life Application (cont.)

4. Oops! Oscar's dad reminds him to think about how much gas he's going to need to run the mower and weed trimmer. If he plans to use $75 in gasoline, how many lawns does Oscar now need to mow to afford his new trumpet? Write and solve an inequality to answer the question.

_____

_____

Raking Leaves

Leslie earns money every fall by raking leaves. To estimate the cost of raking each lawn, Leslie starts by determining the area of the lawn. Once she knows the size of the lawn, she can approximate how long it will take her to rake up the leaves.

5. Here is a map of the first lawn that she is going to rake.

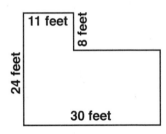

a. What is the area of this lawn?

_____

_____

b. If Leslie can rake 150 square feet in an hour, how long will it take her to rake this lawn? Round your answer to the nearest hundredth.

_____

_____

Name: _____ Date: _____

Unit 1: The Mathematics of Lawn Care

Real-Life Application (cont.)

c. If Leslie charges $12.50 per hour to rake, how much will she earn for raking this lawn?

_____

6. Here is the second lawn Leslie is going to rake:

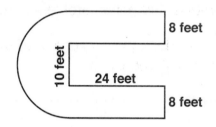

How much will Leslie earn by raking the leaves on this lawn? Show your work.

_____

Shoveling Snow

Kendra has decided to earn money this winter by shoveling the snow from people's driveways. Because it is so cold in the winter, she is thinking hard about how long she has to travel in between homes. Here is a map of the houses on her street. Kendra's home is located at 0.

7. Kendra has been hired to shovel the driveways of house A and house C. She is considering how far she's going to have to walk on a cold morning.

a. How far is house A from Kendra's house? _____

_____

Name: _____ Date: _____

Unit 1: The Mathematics of Lawn Care

Real-Life Application (cont.)

b. How far is house C from Kendra's house? _____

_____

c. How far is house A from house C? _____

_____

d. Write a subtraction problem to represent this situation. _____

e. Explain how you can use absolute values to find the difference between the locations of houses A and C.

_____

_____

_____

8. The following week, Kendra is hired to shovel driveways for house A and house D. Write a subtraction problem to represent the distance between house A and house D, and explain how Kendra can use absolute values to find the difference between the locations of these houses.

_____

_____

_____

_____

_____

_____

9. Finally, Kendra is asked to shovel the driveways of houses E and B. Show how Kendra can use absolute values to find the distance between the locations of these houses.

_____

_____

_____

_____

Unit 2: The Mathematics of Yard Sales

Introduction

Yard sales are a great way to clean out your closets and make some money! Most people love getting a great deal, and many enjoy visiting neighborhood yard sales to find those great bargains. Yard sales are so popular that the second Saturday in August has been designated as *National Yard Sale Day*. According to *Forbes* magazine, during the summer months, there are approximately 165,000 yard sales each week in the United States. These sales attract about 690,000 buyers who will purchase nearly 5 million items, yielding revenue around $4,222,375.

While yard sales can help you make some cash, they do require a lot of work. The seller must sort through their unwanted belongings and decide what is worth selling and what is not. They must price their items so that others will be interested in buying them. They must also make sure that they advertise their sale so that lots of bargain hunters know about it.

The mathematics needed to run a yard sale will be the focus of this unit.

Common Core State Standards

This unit addresses the following Common Core State Standards:

- CCSS.Math.Content.7.NS.A.2a
- CCSS.Math.Content.7.NS.A.2c
- CCSS.Math.Content.7.NS.A.2d
- CCSS.Math.Content.7.EE.A.2

- CCSS.Math.Content.7.EE.B.3
- CCSS.Math.Content.7.EE.B.4a
- CCSS.Math.Content.7.SP.C.5
- CCSS.Math.Content.7.SP.C.7a

Prerequisite Skills

Prior to completing this unit, students should be proficient in the following mathematical skills: (Note: A practice sheet has been provided for each skill listed.)

- Multiplying rational numbers
- Writing and solving equations for a given situation
- Understanding probability

Name: _____ Date: _____

Unit 2: The Mathematics of Yard Sales

Prerequisite Skill Practice—Multiplying Rational Numbers

Directions: Multiply. Write your answer in simplest form when appropriate. The first problem has been worked out as an example.

1. $\dfrac{3}{8} \cdot 4.48$ $$\dfrac{3}{8} \cdot 4.48 = \dfrac{3}{8} \cdot \dfrac{4.48}{1}$$ $$= \dfrac{13.44}{8}$$ $$= 1.68$$	2. $\dfrac{7}{9} \cdot 245.7$
3. $\dfrac{5}{7} \cdot \dfrac{14}{17}$	4. $\dfrac{9}{11} \cdot \dfrac{5}{6}$
5. $2.33 \cdot 15.194$	6. $0.87 \cdot 9.1$
7. $4.5 \cdot \dfrac{13}{15}$	8. $19 \cdot 123.76$

Name: _____ Date: _____

Unit 2: The Mathematics of Yard Sales

Prerequisite Skill Practice—Writing and Solving Equations

Directions: Write and solve an equation for the given situation. Be sure to define your variables. The first problem has been worked out as an example.

1. Josh is half as old as his cousin. If his cousin is 14 years old, how old is Josh? Let j represent Josh's age and c represent his cousin's age. Then $j = \frac{1}{2}c$. Because $c = 14$, then $j = \frac{1}{2} \cdot 14$ or 7. Josh is 7 years old.	2. Bentley weighs $\frac{2}{3}$ as much as Daphne. If Daphne weights 72 pounds, how much does Bentley weigh?
3. A great white shark is four times as long as a man who is 1.6 meters tall. How long is the great white shark?	4. Octavia's sales today were 72% of yesterday's sales. If Octavia's sales from yesterday totaled $635.90, what were her sales today?
5. Wing needs to increase his weight by 12% so that he will weigh enough to wrestle in his desired weight class next year. If Wing currently weighs 108 pounds, how much does he need to weigh next year?	6. A pair of jeans is on sale for 30% off. If the original price of the jeans is $42.60, what is the sale price of the jeans?
7. Sandra has $210.15 in her account, which includes the amount she earned when she sold her bicycle. Sandra plans to donate $\frac{1}{4}$ of the profit from her bicycle sale to charity. If she sold her bicycle for $124, how much will Sandra have in her account after she donates to charity?	8. Xavier sold a total of 89 tickets to the play, which includes the number of tickets he sold to his family. Colton sold the amount of tickets Xavier sold plus 20 percent more than the amount that Xavier sold to his family. If Xavier sold 30 tickets to his family, how many tickets did Colton sell?

Name: _____ Date: _____

Unit 2: The Mathematics of Yard Sales

Prerequisite Skill Practice—Understanding Probability

Directions: Explain whether the given probability means that the event is unlikely, likely, or neither. The first problem has been worked out as an example.

1. The probability that Donna will win the game is $\frac{1}{4}$. Because the probability is closer to 0 than 1, this event is unlikely.	2. The probability that the spinner will land on green is $\frac{8}{9}$.
3. The probability that the six-sided number cube will land on an even number is $\frac{3}{6}$.	4. The probability that Steve will make the free throw is $\frac{11}{15}$.
5. The probability that the coin will land on heads is $\frac{1}{2}$.	6. The probability that the spinner will land on red is $\frac{5}{11}$.
7. The probability that Jane will draw a vowel is $\frac{5}{26}$.	8. The probability that Maria will roll doubles is $\frac{1}{6}$.

Name: _____ Date: _____

Unit 2: The Mathematics of Yard Sales

Real-Life Application

Yard sales are a great way to clean out unwanted items and earn some money. Those who shop at yard sales are always looking for a good deal. It's important to have some mathematical skills when you organize a yard sale so that you can turn a good profit. We will explore some of the mathematics of yard sales in this unit.

Planning and Advertising

Imagine that you are planning to hold a yard sale. You decide to do some research to determine the best time to have the sale and how to advertise it.

1. Your online research shows that people have mixed opinions about what day of the week is best for a yard sale. Some say Friday, others say Saturday, and some even say Thursday or Sunday. You decide to survey your friends and find that four times as many friends suggest that you hold your yard sale on Saturday than those who suggest you hold it on Friday.

    a. Write an equation to represent this situation. Be sure to define your variables.

    _____

    _____

    b. Six of your friends recommended you hold your yard sale on Friday. Use the equation you wrote in #1a to determine the number of friends who suggested you hold your yard sale on Saturday. Show your work.

    _____

    _____

    c. How many friends suggested that you hold your yard sale on Friday or Saturday? Explain how you determined your answer.

    _____

    _____

    _____

Name: _____   Date: _____

Unit 2: The Mathematics of Yard Sales

Real-Life Application (cont.)

2. You decide to purchase some signs to advertise for your yard sale. You find a great service online that will make the signs inexpensively. If you purchase one to three signs, they will cost $5.97 each. If you purchase four or five signs, you will receive a 10% discount on the price of each sign. If you purchase six or more signs, you will receive an 18% discount on the price of each sign.

a. Complete the equation below that can be used to calculate the discounted price for purchasing six or more signs. In the given equation, c represents the original cost of each sign and d represents the discounted cost of each sign.

$$d = c - \boxed{} c$$

b. Simplify the equation from #2a.

_____

c. Compare and contrast the equations in #2a and #2b.

_____

_____

_____

_____

d. You decide to purchase eight signs. Calculate the total cost of the signs. Show your work.

_____

_____

Name: _____ Date: _____

Unit 2: The Mathematics of Yard Sales

Real-Life Application (cont.)

Pricing and Selling Your Items

3. You have gathered a collection of items that you would like to sell, and you need to determine what prices to put on them. The general rule of thumb is that you should price gently used items at $\frac{1}{3}$ of their original selling price and more significantly used items at 10% of their original selling price.

   a. Write an equation that can be used to calculate the yard sale price for gently used items. Be sure to define your variables.

   _____

   _____

   b. Write an equation that can be used to calculate the yard sale price for more significantly used items. Use the same variables as the ones you used in #3a.

   _____

   _____

   c. Use the equations you wrote in #3a and #3b to calculate the yard sale price for the items in the table below. Round your answers to the nearest cent when necessary.

Item	Original Price	Quality	Recommended Yard Sale Price
Lamp	$42.78	Gently used	
Glass pitcher	$12.95	Gently used	
Frame	$32.99	Significantly used	
Toaster	$49.95	Gently used	
Chainsaw	$164.79	Significantly used	

   d. You decide that you would rather not have to deal with dimes, nickels, and pennies. So you decide to round each of the prices you calculated in #3c to the nearest quarter. Complete the table below to show how you will actually price each of the items.

Item	Original Price	Quality	Actual Yard Sale Price
Lamp	$42.78	Gently used	
Glass pitcher	$12.95	Gently used	
Frame	$32.99	Significantly used	
Toaster	$49.95	Gently used	
Chainsaw	$164.79	Significantly used	

Name: _____ Date: _____

Unit 2: The Mathematics of Yard Sales

Real-Life Application (cont.)

4. In your research online, you discover that people sell most of their items before noon and that it is a good idea to offer significant discounts on your items in the afternoon to encourage shoppers to buy them. You decide to make a "discount wheel" that customers can spin to get additional discounts on your already cheap items. A sketch of your "discount wheel" is shown at the right.

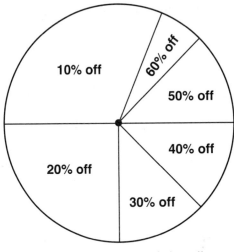

a. Is the probability equally likely that the spinner will land on any one of the discounts? Explain your reasoning.

_____

_____

b. Which discount is the spinner most likely to land on? Explain how you determined your answer.

_____

_____

c. Which discount is the spinner least likely to land on? Explain how you determined your answer.

_____

_____

d. Which discount is the spinner likely to land on $\frac{1}{4}$ of the time? Explain how you determined your answer.

_____

_____

Name: _____ Date: _____

Unit 2: The Mathematics of Yard Sales

Real-Life Application (cont.)

5. Your neighbor sees your spinner and suggests that it would be better if all of the outcomes are equally likely. Design a new spinner in which all of the discounts are equally likely. Explain how you determined your answer.

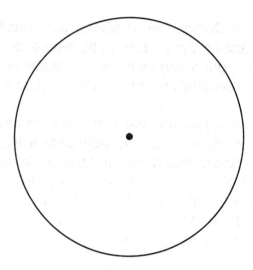

_____

_____

_____

_____

_____

6. Your other neighbor suggests that you allow your customers to roll a six-sided number cube to determine their discount. If they roll a one, then they get a 10% discount. If they roll a two, then they get a 20% discount, and so on.

a. Are all of the discounts equally likely using this model? Explain your reasoning.

_____

_____

_____

b. How does this model compare and contrast with the model in #5?

_____

_____

_____

_____

Unit 3: The Mathematics of Food Pantries

Introduction

Community service is both challenging and rewarding, and it provides a direct positive impact on the lives of people around you. One way to get involved with your community is by working or volunteering at a food pantry. Doing so may require working with ratios and proportions, solving equations, or calculating values using geometry.

Acquiring sufficient food to supply those in need is an essential part of operating a food pantry. Purchasing necessary quantities of food while staying within a strict budget can involve comparing unit prices to obtain the best deals possible. These tasks require an understanding of ratios and proportions, which may also be used for other aspects of running a food pantry.

Issues that might be encountered while working at a food pantry include sufficiently staffing shifts, determining how to close budget gaps, and calculating how to allocate resources. Writing and solving algebraic equations and inequalities can assist in efficiently determining how to solve these and other problems.

Operating a food pantry involves basic geometric calculations. Once food is obtained, it must be properly stored and prepared for distribution to those in need. Loading boxes, fitting supplies in warehouses, and determining delivery areas for drivers require knowledge of geometry.

These are just some of the ways mathematics is encountered when running a charity and will be the focus of this unit as students explore the math used in operating a food pantry.

Common Core State Standards

This unit addresses the following Common Core State Standards:

- CCSS.Math.Content.7.RP.A.3
- CCSS.Math.Content.7.NS.A.2
- CCSS.Math.Content.7.NS.A.3

- CCSS.Math.Content.7.EE.B.4
- CCSS.Math.Content.7.G.B.4
- CCSS.Math.Content.7.G.B.6

Prerequisite Skills

Prior to completing this unit, students should be proficient in the following mathematical skills: (Note: A practice sheet has been provided for each skill listed.)

- Solving problems involving ratios and proportions
- Writing and solving algebraic equations and inequalities
- Calculating values involving perimeter, area, and volume of geometric figures

Name: _____ Date: _____

Unit 3: The Mathematics of Food Pantries

Prerequisite Skill Practice—Ratios and Proportions

Directions: Complete each exercise as indicated. Show your work. The first problem has been worked out as an example.

1. The ratio of volunteers to paid staff at a charity event is 5:2. How many volunteers are present if 14 paid staff are working? $$\frac{5}{2} = \frac{x}{14}$$ $14 \cdot 5 = 2 \cdot x$ $70 = 2x$ $x = 70 \div 2$ $x = 35$ There are 35 volunteers.	**2.** Determine the value of t: $$\frac{32}{t} = \frac{9}{20}$$
3. A motorcycle uses 4 gallons of gas to travel 167 miles. Determine the unit rate of fuel efficiency in miles per gallon.	**4.** Determine the value of r: $$\frac{r}{15} = \frac{40}{21}$$
5. Determine the value of k: $$\frac{3}{8} = \frac{k}{10}$$	**6.** The ratio of boxes of pasta to cans of vegetables at a food bank is 7:4. How many cans of vegetables are available if there are 518 boxes of pasta?
7. Determine the value of d: $$\frac{14}{85} = \frac{98}{d}$$	**8.** The unit price for seedless grapes is $2.79 per pound. What is the price of 4.65 pounds of seedless grapes?

Name: _____   Date: _____

Unit 3: The Mathematics of Food Pantries

Prerequisite Skill Practice—Algebraic Equations and Inequalities

Directions: Complete each exercise as indicated. Show your work. The first problem has been worked out as an example.

1. Solve the following equation: $$6(x - 5) = 72$$ $$\frac{6(x - 5)}{6} = \frac{72}{6}$$ $$x - 5 = 12$$ $$+ 5 = + 5$$ $$x = 17$$	2. The Cupcake of the Month Club costs \$25.00 to join plus \$14.95 per month for delivery of one dozen gourmet cupcakes. Write an equation to represent the total amount, A, paid to be a member of the club for m months.
3. Pens are sold in boxes of 60. An event planner currently has 382 pens in stock but needs at least 1,000 pens for an up-coming event. Write an inequality to help the event planner determine how many boxes of pens, b, to purchase.	4. Solve the following equation: $$0.8x - 3.9 = 5.3$$
5. Solve the following inequality: $$7x + 24 \le 59$$	6. Each can of beans holds 15.5 ounces. There are currently 40 ounces of beans in a pot that can cook a maximum of 96 ounces of beans at a time. Write an inequality to determine how many cans of beans, c, can be safely added to the pot.
7. Solve the following equation: $$-\frac{2}{5}\left(x + \frac{1}{4}\right) = \frac{7}{10}$$	8. Solve the following equation: $$\frac{2}{3}\left(x - 5\frac{1}{4}\right) = 6\frac{7}{8}$$

Name: _____ Date: _____

Unit 3: The Mathematics of Food Pantries

Prerequisite Skill Practice—Perimeter, Area, and Volume

Directions: Complete each exercise as indicated. Show your work. The first problem has been worked out as an example.

1. Determine the exact area of a circle with a diameter of 10 centimeters. Diameter = 10 cm → radius = 5 cm $A = \pi r^2 = \pi(5)^2 = \pi \cdot 25 = 25\pi$ The circle has an exact area of $25\pi\,cm^2$.	**2.** Calculate the surface area of a cube with an edge length of $2\frac{3}{4}$ inches.
3. What is the height of a triangle with an area of 60 square feet and a base measuring 8 feet?	**4.** A right hexagonal prism has a base with an area of 6.28 square meters and a height of 14.75 meters. Compute its volume.
5. The base of a right square prism has an edge length of 3 feet. Compute the surface area of the prism if its height is 5 feet.	**6.** Calculate the exact circumference of a circle with a radius of 48 millimeters.
7. Determine the exact area of a circle with a circumference of 2.8π inches.	**8.** Compute the volume of a box with the following dimensions measured in centimeters: 28.4 • 22 • 9.8

Name: _____ Date: _____

Unit 3: The Mathematics of Food Pantries

Real-Life Application

Being involved with community service is a great way to benefit those around you while truly making a difference and simply feeling good about yourself. One way to get involved is through a food pantry, which is an organization that provides food to those who do not have enough to eat despite often having jobs and a place to live. This unit explores some of the mathematics involved in running a food pantry.

Financing a Food Pantry

The financial component of operating a food pantry can be complicated and requires a good deal of mathematics. This section addresses some of the financial concerns faced by Helping Hands Food Pantry each month.

1. Helping Hands obtains most of the food they distribute to those in need by purchasing bulk quantities from their local food bank. The food pantry purchased 9,426 pounds of food for $65,982.00 last month.

   a. What unit price did Helping Hands pay at the local food bank last month?

   _____

   b. Helping Hands predicts a need for approximately 140,000 pounds of food next year. Assuming the charity continues to purchase their food from the same local food bank for the same unit price calculated in #1a, how much does Helping Hands need to budget for food purchases next year?

   _____

Name: _____ Date: _____

Unit 3: The Mathematics of Food Pantries

Real-Life Application (cont.)

2. Although much of their operating budgets are covered by governmental aid, food pantries rely on donations to make ends meet. In order to continue to provide services to the community, Helping Hands must raise $5,245 per month in donations to fill the budget gap not covered by governmental aid.

a. Helping Hands has a group of loyal individual and corporate donors who give recurring gifts totaling $3,680 per month. In order to fill the remaining budget gap, Helping Hands decides to conduct a fundraising campaign in which they ask local businesses to donate $35 each month in exchange for advertising in the charity's monthly newsletter. Using b to represent the number of local business sponsors, write an equation to determine how many local business sponsors would be needed to fill the gap in their monthly budget not covered by governmental aid or recurring gifts from loyal donors.

_____

b. Solve the equation you wrote in #2a. Interpret your answer in the context of this situation.

_____

_____

Inventory Management

To be effective, food pantries must stock enough food to be able to provide those in need with adequate supplies to keep from going hungry. The questions in this section pertain to managing the inventory at Helping Hands Food Pantry.

3. Helping Hands Food Pantry serves a region containing 126,582 households. Data gathered from that region indicates that 14.22% of households require food assistance. Determine the number of households in the region served by Helping Hands that require food assistance. Explain your reasoning.

_____

_____

Name: _____ Date: _____

Unit 3: The Mathematics of Food Pantries

Real-Life Application (cont.)

4. It takes approximately 4 pounds of food per person each day to avoid going hungry. If there are an average of 3.5 people per household in the region served by Helping Hands, use your answer to #3 to determine how many pounds of food Helping Hands Food Pantry should plan to distribute each week in order to supply every person requiring food assistance in the region with enough food to avoid going hungry. Explain why Helping Hands may not actually need to plan to distribute the full amount of food calculated.

_____

_____

_____

_____

_____

5. Helping Hands Food Pantry pre-packages boxes of food to distribute to the community. Each box is $1\frac{3}{4}$ feet long, $1\frac{1}{4}$ feet wide, and 1 foot high. The organization rents floor space measuring 70 feet by 35 feet in a warehouse to store the boxes. How many boxes can they store in the warehouse if they can store the boxes in stacks of six?

_____

Name: _____ Date: _____

Unit 3: The Mathematics of Food Pantries

Real-Life Application (cont.)

Food Distribution

Although properly budgeting finances and managing inventory are important, food pantries must be able to get their products to the community members in need. This section deals with some of the concerns a food pantry faces when distributing food to the community.

6. To better serve the community, Helping Hands delivers food to those who are unable to get themselves to the distribution center, as long as they are within a 6-mile radius of its headquarters. Each driver can effectively cover an area of 30 square miles. How many drivers are needed for Helping Hands Food Pantry to continue this service?

_____

7. Helping Hands relies on volunteers to help distribute food to the community. Paid staff members spend 96 hours per month assisting with food distribution, and volunteers are asked to work 3-hour shifts to assist. This month, Helping Hands wants to devote more than 150 hours to distributing food.

   a. Using *n* to represent the number of volunteer shifts to be filled, write an inequality to determine how many volunteer shifts need to be filled for Helping Hands to meet their goal of devoting over 150 hours to distributing food this month.

   _____

   b. Solve the inequality you wrote in #7a. Interpret your answer in the context of this situation. Specifically, discuss the number of volunteers that may be needed to meet the desired goal.

   _____

   _____

   _____

Unit 4: The Mathematics of Mechanics

Introduction

The United States is a car-centric society. Unless you live in a big city that has good public transportation, it's difficult to get around without a car. If you have a car, you need to know a good mechanic who can help you keep your car in tip-top shape. Being an auto mechanic can be a good way to earn a living. On average, an auto mechanic makes around $17.65 per hour, which is about $36,710 per year, according to the U.S. Bureau of Labor Statistics.

While auto mechanics do work with their hands, they must also be able to think logically and mathematically. Mechanics must be able to calculate volumes and use a variety of other formulas to ensure that an automobile can function properly. They must use proportional reasoning regularly, as they work with gears and the different systems in the car. For example, it is important to have the right mix of water and antifreeze in a cooling system so that the engine can function efficiently in a variety of temperatures.

These are just some of the ways mathematics is used by mechanics and will be the focus of this unit as students explore the math needed to keep vehicles running safely and efficiently.

Common Core State Standards

This unit addresses the following Common Core State Standards:

- CCSS.Math.Content.7.RP.A.2a
- CCSS.Math.Content.7.RP.A.2b
- CCSS.Math.Content.7.RP.A.2c
- CCSS.Math.Content.7.NS.A.1b
- CCSS.Math.Content.7.NS.A.1c
- CCSS.Math.Content.7.NS.A.1d
- CCSS.Math.Content.7.NS.A.2a

- CCSS.Math.Content.7.NS.A.2b
- CCSS.Math.Content.7.NS.A.2c
- CCSS.Math.Content.7.NS.A.2d
- CCSS.Math.Content.7.NS.A.3
- CCSS.Math.Content.7.EE.B.3
- CCSS.Math.Content.7.EE.B.4a
- CCSS.Math.Content.7.EE.B.4b

Prerequisite Skills

Prior to completing this unit, students should be proficient in the following mathematical skills: (Note: A practice sheet has been provided for each skill listed.)

- Evaluating expressions
- Determining whether quantities have a proportional relationship
- Solving and graphing the solution sets of inequalities

Name: _____　　Date: _____

Unit 4: The Mathematics of Mechanics

Prerequisite Skill Practice—Evaluating Expressions

Directions: Evaluate the expression for the given integer. The first problem has been worked out as an example.

1. $y = \frac{3}{4}x + 9$, for $x = -16$ $y = \frac{3}{4}(-16) + 9$ $= \frac{3}{4}\left(\frac{-16}{1}\right) + 9$ $= \frac{-48}{4} + 9$ $= -12 + 9$ $= -3$	**2.** $a = -\frac{2}{9}b + 13$, for $b = -27$
3. $r = \frac{5}{8}s - 23$, for $s = -64$	**4.** $m = -\frac{5}{6}n - 19$, for $n = -42$
5. $w = \frac{7}{8}x + 21$, for $x = 32$	**6.** $p = -\frac{5}{9}r + 17$, for $r = 18$
7. $k = \frac{2}{3}l - 35$, for $l = 33$	**8.** $q = -\frac{5}{12}r - 25$, for $r = 36$

Name: _____   Date: _____

Unit 4: The Mathematics of Mechanics

Prerequisite Skill Practice—Identifying Proportional Relationships

Directions: Determine whether or not the quantities in the table have a proportional relationship. Explain how you determined your answer. The first problem has been worked out as an example.

1.

x	y
1	3
2	6
3	9
4	12
5	15

The quantities have a proportional relationship because the ratio of the y values to their corresponding x values is constant.

That is $\frac{3}{1} = \frac{6}{2} = \frac{9}{3} = \frac{12}{4} = \frac{15}{5}$.

2.

x	y
1	5
2	10
3	15
4	20
5	25

3.

x	y
1	1
2	2
3	4
4	8
5	16

4.

x	y
1	4
3	12
6	24
10	40
20	80

5.

x	y
2	1
4	1
6	2
8	3
10	5

6.

x	y
1	$\frac{1}{2}$
2	1
3	$\frac{3}{2}$
4	2
5	$\frac{5}{2}$

Name: _____ Date: _____

Unit 4: The Mathematics of Mechanics

Prerequisite Skill Practice—Solving and Graphing Inequalities

Directions: Solve the given inequality and then graph the solution set on the number line. The first problem has been worked out as an example.

1. $-3x - 5 \geq 10$

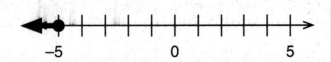

$$-3x - 5 \geq 10$$
$$-3x - 5 + 5 \geq 10 + 5$$
$$\frac{-3x}{-3} \geq \frac{15}{-3}$$
$$x \leq -5$$

2. $2m + 7 > -3$

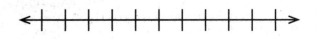

3. $-5b + 8 < 3$

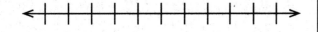

4. $-9a + 2 \leq -16$

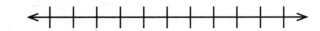

5. $-7p - 13 \geq -20$

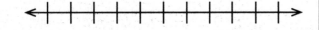

6. $4s - 7 < 5$

Name: _____ Date: _____

Unit 4: The Mathematics of Mechanics

Real-Life Application

Cooling Systems

The engine of a car generates a lot of heat when it is in operation. It is important to keep the engine cool so that it does not seize. Seizing can occur when the engine overheats and pistons become welded to the cylinders. The result is an engine that does not work.

Most cars have a liquid cooling system. The liquid passes through the engine and absorbs the heat generated by the engine. It then leaves the engine and passes through the radiator where the heat in the liquid is transferred to the air and away from the engine.

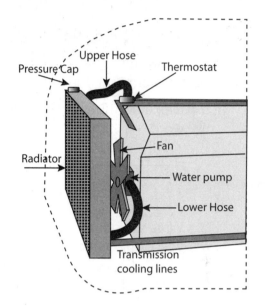

Freezing/Boiling Points of Liquid Coolants

Water can be used in a car's cooling system. However, it freezes at too high a temperature. So most of the time, mechanics put a mixture of water and antifreeze in the cooling system. The table below shows different liquids used in car cooling systems and their freezing and boiling points.

Liquid	Freezing Point (°C)	Boiling Point (°C)
Water	0	100
50/50 mix of antifreeze and water	−37	106
70/30 mix of antifreeze and water	−55	113

1. The formula for converting degrees Celsius to degrees Fahrenheit is $F = \frac{9}{5}C + 32$. Use this formula to calculate the freezing and boiling points of the liquids in the table to degrees Fahrenheit.

Liquid	Freezing Point (°F)	Boiling Point (°F)
Water		
50/50 mix of antifreeze and water		
70/30 mix of antifreeze and water		

Name: _____ Date: _____

Unit 4: The Mathematics of Mechanics

Real-Life Application (cont.)

Cooling System Capacities

2. Cooling systems have different capacities. Let's say you want to put a 70/30 mix of cooling liquid in a car that you are working on. The car has a 14-quart capacity cooling system.

a. Calculate how many quarts of antifreeze you will need for your solution. Show your work.

_____

b. Write an equation that could be used to determine the number of quarts of antifreeze you would need for any capacity cooling system. Be sure to define your variables.

_____

_____

c. What is the constant of proportionality in the equation you wrote in #2b? Explain how you determined your answer.

_____

_____

_____

d. Calculate how many quarts of water you will need for your solution. Show your work.

_____

e. Write an equation that could be used to determine the number of quarts of water you would need for any capacity cooling system. Be sure to define your variables.

_____

_____

f. What is the constant of proportionality in the equation you wrote in #2e? Explain how you determined your answer.

_____

_____

Name: _____ Date: _____

Unit 4: The Mathematics of Mechanics

Real-Life Application (cont.)

3. The table below shows the relationship between the capacity of the cooling system and freezing point of the cooling liquid when five quarts of antifreeze are part of the mixture of antifreeze and water.

Cooling System Capacity (quarts)	10	11	12	13	14	15	16	17
Freezing Point (°F)	−34	−23	−15	−9	−5	0	2	5

a. Are the capacity and freezing point in a proportional relationship? Explain how you determined your answer.

_____

_____

_____

_____

b. Graph the data in the table on the grid below.

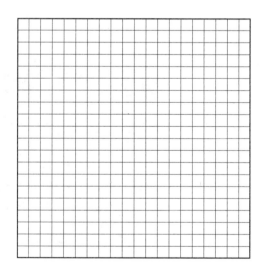

c. Explain how the graph you made in #3b supports your answer to #3a.

_____

_____

_____

Name: _____ Date: _____

Unit 4: The Mathematics of Mechanics

Real-Life Application (cont.)

Pressure and Cooling Systems

4. In addition to adding antifreeze to water to reduce the freezing point and increase the boiling point, you can also increase the pressure in the coolant system to further increase the boiling point. The table shows the relationship between the pressure measured in pounds per square inch (psi) and the boiling point for a cooling liquid that is a 50/50 antifreeze and water mixture.

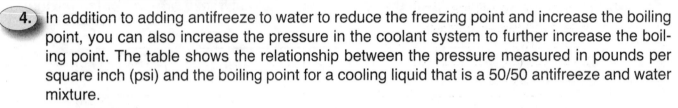

Pressure (psi)	0	3	5	10	12	15	20
Boiling Point (°F)	222	231	237	252	258	267	282

a. Are the pressure and boiling point in a proportional relationship? Explain how you determined your answer.

_____

_____

_____

b. Graph the data in the table on the grid below.

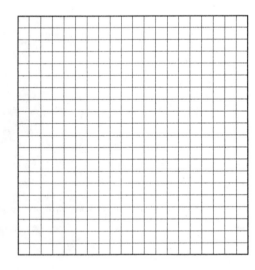

c. Explain how the graph you made in #4b supports your answer to #4a.

_____

_____

Name: _____ Date: _____

Unit 4: The Mathematics of Mechanics

Real-Life Application (cont.)

d. Calculate the ratios for the change between the values of the boiling points over the change in the values of the pressure. What does this tell you about the relationship between the two quantities?

_____

_____

_____

e. Draw a line through the points on the graph. Where does the line cross the *y*-axis?

_____

f. Use your answers to #4d and #4e to write an equation that represents the relationship between the pressure and the boiling point of the cooling liquid. Be sure to define your variables.

_____

_____

g. Let's say that you would like to apply enough pressure so that the boiling point of the cooling liquid is at most 258°F. Write an inequality that represents this situation.

_____

_____

h. Solve the inequality that you wrote in #4g. Then graph the solution on the number line.

i. Explain what the solution that you calculated in #4h means in this context.

_____

_____

_____

Unit 5: The Mathematics of Car Sales

Introduction

Are you interested in cars? Do you like people? If so, you may be an excellent car salesperson.

A car salesperson is usually paid by commission, which means that their pay is dependent on the number of cars that they sell. Because of this, car salespeople usually work evenings and weekends when they have the best opportunity to meet with customers. The salesperson needs to know about all different kinds of vehicles and be able to match a customer to the right vehicle. Convincing customers to return the next time they need a car and to refer their friends is an important aspect of the car salesperson's job. Understanding customers, sales strategies, types of vehicles, and the car sales market requires a significant amount of mathematical thinking.

This type of sales job is different from other sales jobs because the price of cars is sometimes negotiable. The car salesperson needs strong mental math skills to navigate the negotiation, taking into account what the customer is willing to pay and the costs of the dealership.

This unit will focus on a number of mathematical concepts that a car salesperson uses to understand the market, customers, vehicles, and the minimum price for a new car.

Common Core State Standards

This unit addresses the following Common Core State Standards:

- CCSS.Math.Content.7.RP.A.1
- CCSS.Math.Content.7.RP.A.2A
- CCSS.Math.Content.7.RP.A.2D
- CCSS.Math.Content.7.RP.A.3
- CCSS.Math.Content.7.EE.A.2

- CCSS.Math.Content.7.EE.B.3
- CCSS.Math.Content.7.SP.A.2
- CCSS.Math.Content.7.SP.C.6
- CCSS.Math.Content.7.SP.C.8A
- CCSS.Math.Content.7.SP.C.8B

Prerequisite Skills

Prior to completing this unit, students should be proficient in the following mathematical skills: (Note: A practice sheet has been provided for each skill listed.)

- Determining whether two quantities have a proportional relationship
- Writing equivalent expressions for percent problems
- Representing sample spaces for compound events

Name: _____ Date: _____

Unit 5: The Mathematics of Car Sales

Prerequisite Skill Practice—Identifying Proportional Relationships

Directions: Determine if the graph represents quantities that are in a proportional relationship. Explain your reasoning. The first problem has been worked out as an example.

1. 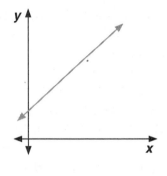 No, the quantities are not proportional. Although the graph is a straight line, it doesn't go through the origin.	**2.** 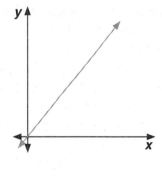
3. 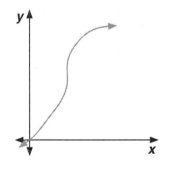	**4.** 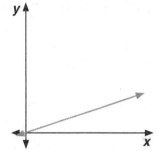
5. 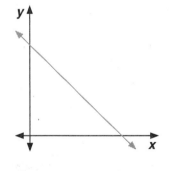	**6.** 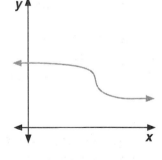
7. 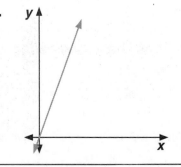	**8.** 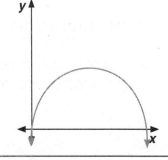

Name: _____ Date: _____

Unit 5: The Mathematics of Car Sales

Prerequisite Skill Practice—Equivalent Percent Expressions

Directions: For each of the following, write two equivalent expressions for the given percent problem. The first problem has been done as an example.

1. A number, n, has been decreased by 40%. $n - 0.40n = 0.60n$	**2.** A number, n, has been increased by 10%.
3. A number, n, has been increased by 78%.	**4.** A number, n, has been decreased by 14%.
5. A number, n, has been decreased by 99%.	**6.** A number, n, has been increased by 150%.
7. A number, n, has been increased by 22.5%.	**8.** A number, n, has been decreased by 1%.
9. A number, n, has been decreased by 42.5%.	**10.** A number, n, has been increased by 6.25%.

Name: _____   Date: _____

Unit 5: The Mathematics of Car Sales

Prerequisite Skill Practice—Sample Spaces

Directions: For each of the following, identify the outcomes in the sample space that compose the event. The first problem has been done as an example.

1. Event: rolling a six-sided number cube and flipping a coin
 	
    1-H, 2-H, 3-H, 4-H, 5-H, 6-H
    1-T, 2-T, 3-T, 4-T, 5-T, 6-T
	2. Event: flipping 2 coins

3. Event: rolling 2 six-sided number cubes	**4.** Event: selecting one color from red, blue, yellow, green and picking a number from 1 through 5
5. Event: choosing a size (S, M, L) and selecting an article of clothing (shirt, pants, socks).	**6.** Event: playing rock-paper-scissors with a friend

Name: _____   Date: _____

Unit 5: The Mathematics of Car Sales

Real-Life Application

Chuck is a car salesman who earns money based on the number and type of cars that he sells. In order to develop his sales strategies and make as much money as he can, Chuck analyzes all of the data he has about who buys cars.

Sales Calls

When Chuck first started selling cars, he didn't have any customers. Therefore, he began by "cold calling" people in the hopes of gaining some new customers. This strategy involves calling people randomly to try and set appointments with them. The following graph displays the success rate of cold calling.

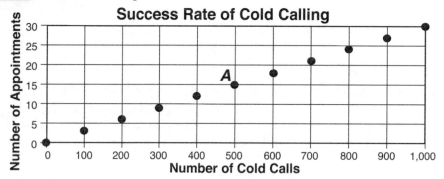

Success Rate of Cold Calling

(y-axis: Number of Appointments, x-axis: Number of Cold Calls)

1. Help Chuck to analyze this graph.

   a. Is the relationship between the number of cold calls and the number of appointments proportional? Explain how you determined your answer.

   _____

   _____

   b. Explain what point *A* means. _____

   _____

   c. What is the rate of success of making appointments from cold calls?

   _____

   d. Would you recommend that Chuck make cold calls to make appointments to sell cars? Explain how you determined your answer.

   _____

   _____

   _____

Name: _____ Date: _____

Unit 5: The Mathematics of Car Sales

Real-Life Application (cont.)

When Chuck starts selling cars, he starts to get referrals, which is when his new customers recommend his services to their friends who are interested in buying a car. The success rate of referral calls is represented in this graph.

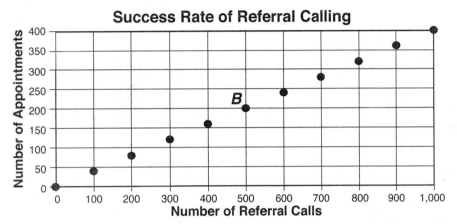

2. Analyze how the success rate for referral calls is different from cold calls.

a. Is the relationship between the number of referral calls and the number of appointments proportional? Explain how you determined your answer.

_____

_____

_____

b. Explain what point *B* means. _____

_____

c. What is the rate of success of making appointments from referral calls?

_____

3. If Chuck wants to set up 25 appointments for the following week, how many cold calls would he need to make? How many referral calls would he need to make?

_____

_____

Name: _____ Date: _____

Unit 5: The Mathematics of Car Sales

Real-Life Application (cont.)

Predicting Sales

In addition to understanding the best way to make sales appointments, a car salesperson also must understand the customers. Chuck randomly selected a day of the week and collected the following data from the customers who visited the dealership throughout the day:

Purchased a car	Did not purchase a car
卌 卌 卌 |||	卌 卌 卌 卌 卌 ||

4. Based on the data Chuck collected, approximate the probability that a customer visiting the dealership purchases a car.

_____

5. Of the 1,575 customers who visited the car dealership during the month, how many customers can Chuck expect to purchase a car?

_____

6. Chuck finds that only 510 customers purchased cars during the month. Why might the actual number of customers who purchased a car have been different from the prediction for the month?

_____

_____

Vehicle Options

When a customer comes to meet with Chuck at the dealership, Chuck has to make good use of the customer's time. This means that Chuck has to understand the cars that the dealership has in the lot and be able to match the customer with the car that s/he wants. If the dealership does not have what a customer wants, Chuck has to find it. Here are the different features available in the cars.

Model Type	Transmission Type	Color
Coupe	Manual	Black
Minivan	Automatic	Red
Sedan		Silver
SUV		White
Truck		

Name: _____ Date: _____

Unit 5: The Mathematics of Car Sales

Real-Life Application (cont.)

7. How many different cars are there for a customer to select? Use a list, table, or tree diagram to represent the sample space.

8. If a customer randomly selects a vehicle to test drive, what is the likelihood that it is red with an automatic transmission?

_____

Sales Price

Finally, Chuck has to work with customers to agree on a sales price. This can be quite a challenge, since the final price has to be accepted by the customer and the dealership management.

9. The dealership pays a certain price for each of the vehicles on their lot. They call this the invoice price. Chuck wants to sell a car for at least 7% over invoice.

a. Write an expression that uses addition to represent the sales price that Chuck is willing to offer.

_____

b. Write an expression that uses only multiplication to represent the sales price that Chuck is willing to offer.

_____

c. Are the expressions in #9a and #9b equivalent? Explain how you determined your answer.

_____

_____

d. If Chuck's dealership paid $23,549 for a vehicle, at what price would Chuck be willing to sell it?

_____

Unit 6: The Mathematics of Marketing

Introduction

Marketing is essential to the growth and success of any business. Because marketing managers play a direct role in earning profits for their companies, they are well compensated for their efforts. They earn a median salary of $127,130. In return, marketers must excel in a variety of mathematics. Ratios and proportions can be used to enlarge advertisements to fit on billboards, scale drawings and geometry may be involved when working to increase brand awareness and recognition, and basic statistics is useful in tracking the effectiveness of marketing campaigns.

Advertising plays the largest role of any single component in the field of marketing. Making informed decisions about what, when, where, and how to advertise requires the ability to understand unit rates, work with ratios and proportions, and interpret statistics. It takes a solid, well-rounded mathematical background to run a strong advertising campaign.

Building brand awareness and recognition is also essential to the success of a business. In particular, marketers work with ratios, proportions, and scale drawings to get a company logo into the public eye and to get potential customers thinking about the brand.

Market research involves gathering and analyzing data about what types of products have the potential to be sold to which customers in various regions. Statistics is the fundamental tool used in market research. Having a clear understanding of statistics, particularly how to gather meaningful data and produce useful results, is absolutely essential to market research.

These are just some of the ways mathematics applies to the field of marketing and will be the focus of this unit as students explore the math used in marketing.

Common Core State Standards

This unit addresses the following Common Core State Standards:

- CCSS.Math.Content.7.RP.A.1
- CCSS.Math.Content.7.RP.A.3
- CCSS.Math.Content.7.EE.B.4
- CCSS.Math.Content.7.G.A.1
- CCSS.Math.Content.7.G.B.6
- CCSS.Math.Content.7.SP.A.1
- CCSS.Math.Content.7.SP.A.2
- CCSS.Math.Content.7.SP.C.6

Prerequisite Skills

Prior to completing this unit, students should be proficient in the following mathematical skills: (Note: A practice sheet has been provided for each skill listed.)

- Solving problems involving ratios, proportions, and scale drawings
- Calculating values involving percents
- Working with basic probability and statistics

Name: _____ Date: _____

Unit 6: The Mathematics of Marketing

Prerequisite Skill Practice—Ratios, Proportions, and Scale Drawings

Directions: Complete each exercise as indicated. Show your work. The first problem has been worked out as an example.

---

1. On a city map, 1 inch represents $\frac{3}{4}$ mile. What is the actual distance between two points that are $5\frac{1}{2}$ inches apart on the map?

$$\frac{1}{\frac{3}{4}} = \frac{5\frac{1}{2}}{x} \rightarrow x \cdot 1 = \frac{3}{4} \cdot \frac{11}{2}$$

$$\rightarrow x = \frac{33}{8} \text{ or } 4\frac{1}{8}$$

The two points are $4\frac{1}{8}$ miles apart.

3. Determine the value of g:

$$\frac{g}{35} = \frac{82}{45}$$

---

2. An ad in a newsletter measures $2\frac{1}{2}$ inches by $1\frac{1}{2}$ inches and costs \$60. What is the unit price per square inch?

4. For a particular company, the ratio of people who make online purchases to those who purchase from a retail store is 8:3. How many people make online purchases if 471 people make purchases from a retail store?

---

5. The ratio of male to female customers in a store is 3:4. How many customers are in the store if 51 males are shopping?

6. An architect's drawing indicates a scale of 1 cm = 3 ft. Calculate the area of a wall that is represented by a rectangle measuring 8 cm by $3\frac{1}{2}$ cm.

---

7. What is the price per egg if $2\frac{1}{2}$ dozen eggs cost \$4.20?

8. Determine the value of k:

$$\frac{7}{12} = \frac{k}{19}$$

Name: _____ Date: _____

Unit 6: The Mathematics of Marketing

Prerequisite Skill Practice—Percents

Directions: Complete each exercise as indicated. Show your work. The first problem has been worked out as an example.

1. What is 35% of 72% of 380? $0.35 \cdot 0.72 \cdot 380 = 95.76$	2. What percent of $56\frac{1}{8}$ is $134\frac{7}{10}$?
3. A newspaper cuts its classified ad price from $40 to $34 during the summer. What is the percent decrease in price?	4. What is the total amount paid for an item costing $89.95 if sales tax is 7%?
5. A furniture salesman earns $1,075 per month plus 6.5% commission on the value of furniture sold for the month. What value of furniture must be sold for the salesman to earn $4,000 for the month?	6. A woman estimates that her car is 250 feet away. The car is actually 273 feet away. What is the percent error in the woman's estimation?
7. Compute $\frac{1}{5}$ of 1% of 2,750.	8. The bill for a couple eating dinner in a restaurant is $62.55. The couple uses a discount card that takes 15% off their bill. After the discount, sales tax of 6% is added to the amount left. What is the final amount due for dinner?

Name: _____ Date: _____

Unit 6: The Mathematics of Marketing

Prerequisite Skill Practice—Probability and Statistics

Directions: Complete each exercise as indicated. Show your work. The first problem has been worked out as an example.

1. In a survey of 2,430 iPhone™ users, 119 indicated they would be interested in switching to an Android™ device. To the nearest tenth, what percent of all iPhone™ users do you expect to be interested in switching to an Android™ device? $$\frac{119}{2430} \approx 0.04897 \approx 4.9\%$$ Approximately 4.9% of iPhone™ users are expected to be interested in switching to an Android™ device.	2. In a random sample of 300 students in a high school, 72 said math is their favorite subject. Based on this survey, how many of the 1,492 students in the high school do you expect would consider math to be their favorite subject?
3. Based on probability, which is the least likely event: flipping tails on a coin toss, rolling a 3 on a number cube, or guessing the answer to a multiple-choice test question with 4 possible answers?	4. Explain why surveying a group of business executives who own private planes would not be ideal for determining spending habits of an average middle-class family.
5. In a first-grade classroom, the girls have an average height of 44 inches with a mean absolute deviation of 6 inches, and the boys have an average height of 42 inches with a mean absolute deviation of 3 inches. Is it reasonable to conclude that, on average, the girls are definitely taller than the boys? Explain your answer.	6. If 81% of randomly sampled college students play online games, explain why it is not correct to assume that exactly 81 out of every 100 college students play online games.

Name: _____ Date: _____

Unit 6: The Mathematics of Marketing

Real-Life Application

Successful marketing requires a good deal of mathematics. Arithmetic, proportional reasoning, algebra, geometry, and statistics all play roles in marketing campaigns. This unit explores some of the mathematics encountered in the world of marketing.

Advertising

One of the biggest aspects of marketing is advertising a business to attract customers. A variety of media options exist, including billboards, online ads, television commercials, and radio spots. This section focuses on potential issues related to advertising a business.

1. Billboards can be used to advertise a business to a large number of potential customers in a specific geographic area. They are available for both indoor and outdoor spaces in a wide variety of sizes and styles. Prices also vary greatly, and many unique options may fit within a given budget.

   Which is the better deal based solely on unit price per square foot: a $10\frac{1}{2}$ ft x $22\frac{1}{2}$ ft billboard costing $1,075 per month; or a 14 ft x 48 ft billboard costing $3,125 per month?

   _____

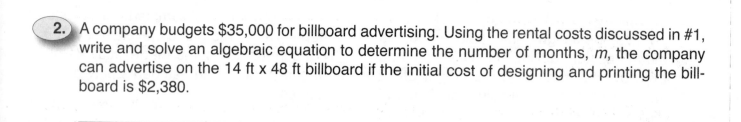

2. A company budgets $35,000 for billboard advertising. Using the rental costs discussed in #1, write and solve an algebraic equation to determine the number of months, m, the company can advertise on the 14 ft x 48 ft billboard if the initial cost of designing and printing the billboard is $2,380.

   _____

   _____

Name: _____ Date: _____

Unit 6: The Mathematics of Marketing

Real-Life Application (cont.)

3. A company purchases online advertising space on a website. The company's banner ad is one of a group from which a randomly selected ad is displayed each time the home page of the website is visited. To determine how many potential customers see the banner ad, the company records which ad appears on 200,000 visits to the home page of the website.

a. The company's ad appears 5,280 times during the study. The website receives 1,750,000 visits to its home page each day. Based on these figures, how many potential customers can the company expect will see the banner ad over the course of 4 weeks? Use mathematics to support your answer.

_____

b. One of the biggest dangers with statistics is misinterpreting results. Explain why your answer to #3a may not provide an accurate estimate of the number of potential customers the company will attract through its online banner advertisement despite the accuracy of the mathematics involved.

_____

_____

_____

4. CalculoCorp's advertising budget was $75,000 last year. In an effort to boost sales, the company decides to increase its advertising budget for this year.

a. CalculoCorp considers increasing its advertising budget to $95,250 this year. What would be the percent increase in the company's advertising budget from last year if they made that change? Support your answer using mathematics.

_____

Name: _____ Date: _____

Unit 6: The Mathematics of Marketing

Real-Life Application (cont.)

b. CalculoCorp wants to boost sales by 4% this year. The company's historical records indicate that each percent increase in advertising expenditures leads to an increase of $\frac{1}{10}$ % in sales. Determine the amount CalculoCorp would need to spend on advertising this year to achieve the desired 4% increase in sales. Use mathematics to support your answer.

_____

Brand Awareness and Recognition

Another important aspect of marketing is building brand awareness and recognition. The more people are exposed to a company's branding tactics, the more recognizable the business becomes, leading to an increase in customers. This section looks at some of the mathematics that may be encountered during the corporate branding process.

5. A new business displays its logo on the wall above its front door. The outline of the logo is a right triangle with dimensions as shown in the figure below.

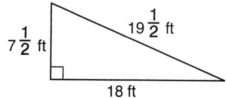

$7\frac{1}{2}$ ft

$19\frac{1}{2}$ ft

18 ft

The company now wants to print standard one-sided business cards measuring $3\frac{1}{2}$ in. x 2 in. on which a scaled-down version of the logo will be displayed.

a. If the logo is printed on the business cards using a scale in which $\frac{1}{8}$ in. represents 1 ft, calculate the lengths of each side of the triangle printed on the business card.

_____

Name: _____ Date: _____

Unit 6: The Mathematics of Marketing

Real-Life Application (cont.)

b. Using the dimensions obtained in #5a, about how much area remains on the business card for content such as contact information and store hours?

_____

Market Research

In order for a product to be profitable for a company, it needs to be affordable, interesting, and useful to potential customers. Companies often conduct extensive research to determine whether a new product is worth developing or an existing product should simply be abandoned altogether. This section explores some of the basic mathematics that can be applied to market research to help make these and other business decisions.

6. A technology company assigns a research team to help decide whether or not to sell a new graphing calculator designed for use on college entrance exams. The research team plans to gather and analyze data collected from a survey of 1,000 randomly selected individuals to help make that decision. Determine whether or not each of the following groups of individuals would provide meaningful results, and explain your reasoning: a) journalists; b) mathematicians; and c) high school students.

_____

_____

_____

7. Companies may opt to research the results of selling a new product or service to a relatively small test market before deciding whether or not to progress to large-scale distribution. A new wireless service was tested in a market of 2,775,000 potential customers, and 74,925 individuals signed up for the service. In order to be profitable on a national level, at least 4,200,000 customers must sign up for the new service if the company makes it available to the masses. Based on the test-market results, would you expect the wireless service to be profitable if it can be made available to a national market of 185,250,000 potential customers? Justify your answer using mathematics.

_____

_____

_____

_____

Unit 7: The Mathematics of Architecture

Introduction

An architect is a person who designs and plans a building and then oversees its construction. They must take many things under consideration when designing a building, including its purpose, location, and the budget for its construction. Architects must be creative and intelligent as they blend art and academics in their designs. Their efforts can earn them a median salary of $73,090.

The Egyptian named Imhotep is considered to be one of the first architects and is probably most well-known for designing the Step Pyramid of Djoser. There have been many other famous architects throughout history. From Gustav Eiffel who is known for the Eiffel Tower in Paris to Eero Saarinen who is known for the Gateway Arch in St. Louis, many architects and their firms have been made famous by the buildings that they designed.

Architects use a lot of mathematics in their work. They must be especially adept in the area of geometry, as their work requires them to be able to accurately calculate area, volume, and angle measures. These are just some of the ways architects use mathematics and will be the focus in this unit.

Common Core State Standards

This unit addresses the following Common Core State Standards:

- CCSS.Math.Content.7.NS.A.2
- CCSS.Math.Content.7.NS.A.3
- CCSS.Math.Content.7.EE.B.3
- CCSS.Math.Content.7.EE.B.4
- CCSS.Math.Content.7.G.A.1

- CCSS.Math.Content.7.G.A.2
- CCSS.Math.Content.7.G.A.3
- CCSS.Math.Content.7.G.B.5
- CCSS.Math.Content.7.G.B.6

Prerequisite Skills

Prior to completing this unit, students should be proficient in the following mathematical skills: (Note: A practice sheet has been provided for each skill listed.)

- Drawing geometric shapes, including right rectangular prisms and pyramids
- Calculating dimensions for a scale model
- Using facts about complementary, supplementary, and adjacent angles to calculate angle measures

Name: _____   Date: _____

Unit 7: The Mathematics of Architecture

Prerequisite Skill Practice—Drawing Geometric Shapes

Directions: Use a straight edge to sketch and label the geometric shape that is described. If it is not possible to draw the shape that is described, explain why not. The first problem has been done as an example.

1. A triangle with side lengths of 2 cm, 3cm, and 7 cm It is not possible to draw a triangle with these dimensions because the sum of the lengths of the two smaller sides is not greater than the length of the third side.	2. A triangle with side lengths of 8.2 ft, 9.1 ft, and 10.4 ft
3. A right rectangular prism with a length of 5 in., a width of 3.5 in., and a height of 8 in.	4. A cube with side lengths of 9 m, 8.9 m, and 9.1 m
5. A right square pyramid with side length of the base of 22 mm and height of 49 mm	6. A triangle with angle measures of 32°, 87°, and 71°

Name: _____　Date: _____

Unit 7: The Mathematics of Architecture

Prerequisite Skill Practice—Calculating Dimensions of Scale Models

Directions: Calculate the dimensions for a scale model given the original dimensions and the scale. The first problem has been worked out as an example.

1. Original dimensions: 273 ft by 486 ft Scale: 1 mm = 3 ft $\dfrac{1\ mm}{3\ ft} = \dfrac{x}{273\ ft} \rightarrow \dfrac{(3\ ft)(x)}{3\ ft} = \dfrac{(1\ mm)(273\ ft)}{3\ ft}$ $x = 91\ mm$ $\dfrac{1\ mm}{3\ ft} = \dfrac{x}{486\ ft} \rightarrow \dfrac{(3\ ft)(x)}{3\ ft} = \dfrac{(1\ mm)(486\ ft)}{3\ ft}$ $x = 162\ mm$ The dimensions of the model are 91 mm by 162 mm.	2. Original dimensions: 87 m by 42 m Scale: 1 cm = 2 m
3. Original dimensions: 112 yd by 372 yd Scale: 1 in. = 4 yd	4. Original dimensions: 2 in. by 9 in. Scale: 1 m = 0.5 in.
5. Original dimensions: 98.5 m by 135.2 m Scale: 1 cm = 10 m	6. Original dimensions: 8.3 cm by 4.9 cm Scale: 1 ft = 0.1 cm

Name: _____ Date: _____

Unit 7: The Mathematics of Architecture

Prerequisite Skill Practice—Complementary, Supplementary, and Adjacent Angles

Directions: Calculate the unknown angle measure. Explain how you determined your answer. The first problem has been worked out as an example.

1. 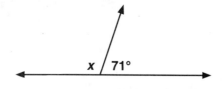 Because the angles form a straight angle, they are supplementary. The sum of their measures is 180°. So $x = 180° - 71°$ or 109°.	**2.** 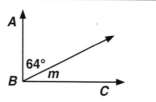 $m\angle ABC = 90°$
3. 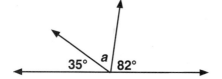	**4.** 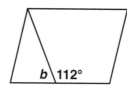
5. 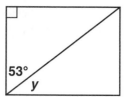	**6.** 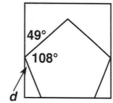
7. An angle has a measure of 29°. What is the measure of its complement?	**8.** An angle has a measure of 136°. What is the measure of its supplement?

Name: _____ Date: _____

Unit 7: The Mathematics of Architecture

Real-Life Application

Being an architect is a good way to combine creativity and mathematics. And, with a median salary of about $73,000 a year, it's also a good way to make a living. We will explore some of the mathematics of architecture in this unit.

Designing a Building

Imagine that you are an architect who works for a firm that has been hired by a company to build a pyramid that will house its employees.

1. Make a sketch of a square pyramid.

2. The company that hired your firm would like for their pyramid to be $\frac{3}{4}$ the size of the Great Pyramid of Giza. The image below shows the original dimensions of the Great Pyramid of Giza. Calculate the dimensions of the base and the height of pyramid that your firm will build. Show your work.

_____

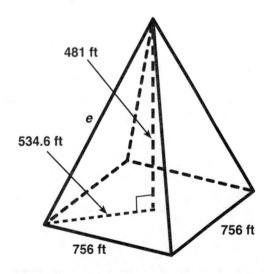

Name: _____ Date: _____

Unit 7: The Mathematics of Architecture

Real-Life Application (cont.)

3. You and your officemate need to determine the length of the edge of the Great Pyramid of Giza so that you can determine the length of the edge of your pyramid. It is denoted by *e* in the image in #2.

    a. Your officemate calculates *e* and gets two different answers. The first time, she gets 719.1 feet, and the second time, she gets 1,019.1 feet. Which calculation is correct? Explain how you determined your answer.

_____

_____

_____

_____

_____

_____

    b. Use your answer to #3a to calculate the edge of your pyramid. Show your work.

_____

Name: _____ Date: _____

Unit 7: The Mathematics of Architecture

Real-Life Application (cont.)

4. You need to make a scale drawing of the pyramid that your firm will build, and it must fit on the next page.

   a. Determine the scale you will use and explain how you determined your answer.

   _____

   _____

   _____

   _____

   _____

   b. Calculate the dimensions of your scale model. Show your work.

   _____

   _____

Name: _____   Date: _____

Unit 7: The Mathematics of Architecture

Real-Life Application (cont.)

c. Use a ruler to draw your scale model.

Name: _____ Date: _____

Unit 7: The Mathematics of Architecture

Real-Life Application (cont.)

5. If one story of a building is about 10 feet, how many stories can your pyramid have? Explain how you determined your answer.

_____

_____

_____

_____

6. The company that hired your firm has some concern about the shape of the floor of each story. Should they be concerned? What will the shape of the floor be? Explain how you determined your answer.

_____

_____

_____

_____

7. Your design includes a set of parallel walls on each floor that are perpendicular to the base of the pyramid and about 8 feet from the outer edge of the floor. Make a sketch of and describe the shape of these walls. Explain how you determined your answer.

_____

_____

_____

_____

Name: _____   Date: _____

Unit 7: The Mathematics of Architecture

Real-Life Application (cont.)

8. You plan for the sides of the pyramid to be windows. If the slant height of the pyramid, denoted by *s* on the image below, is 458.8 feet, how much glass will be needed for all four sides of the pyramid? Show your work.

_____

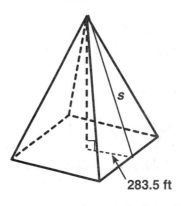

283.5 ft

9. You would like to make the windows using a design that is similar to the one used by I.M. Pei on the Louvre Pyramid. The windows at the base will be equilateral triangles. Then the rest of the windows will be rhombi. You need to determine what the measures of the obtuse angles in the rhombi will be, as denoted by *o* in the image. Explain how you determined your answer.

_____

_____

_____

_____

_____

_____

_____

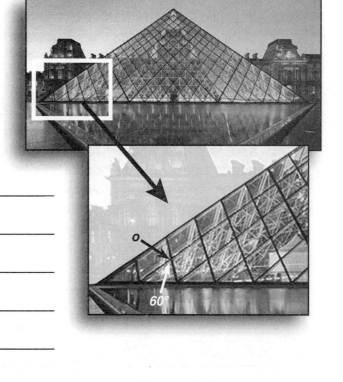

Name: _____ Date: _____

Unit 7: The Mathematics of Architecture

Real-Life Application (cont.)

10. Your officemate thinks it would be better to use a design similar to the one used by Mark C. Hartz on the Memphis Pyramid. In this design, most of the windows would be rectangles.

    a. What other shapes of windows are used in this design?

       _____

       _____

       _____

       _____

    b. You calculate the measure of the angle of the vertex of one of the windows on the side to be 35°. You then explain to your officemate that the measure of the angle of the window marked with an *x* in the diagram is 145°. Your officemate argues that you are wrong and that the angle marked with *x* has a measure of 55° because each of the angles in a rectangle has a measure of 90°. What is the correct angle measure? Explain how you determined your answer.

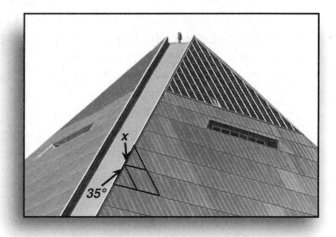

_____

_____

_____

_____

_____

_____

Unit 8: The Mathematics of Nursing

Introduction

Anyone who has been hospitalized appreciates the hard work of nurses. Registered nurses (RNs) work with other health care professionals to provide patients with physical exams, administer medications, interpret patient information and coordinate patient care, educate patients and the community, provide emotional support to patients and their family members, and conduct research in support of improved nursing practices. The median annual salary for this job was $65,470 in 2012 (Bureau of Labor Statistics).

To be a nurse, one must have at least an associate's degree, although many registered nurses have bachelor's and master's degrees. Every nursing program requires a math course and success on a math test in order to graduate. The focus on mathematics in training is due to the amount of math that a nurse must be able to complete in high-pressure situations when lives are on the line.

Nurses use mathematics on a daily basis. They calculate dosages for medication. Giving the wrong amount of medication to a patient could be deadly. They also deal in probabilities, including the likelihood of a patient experiencing a side effect from medication.

This unit will focus on a number of mathematical concepts that a nurse uses to dispense medications safely to patients, understand the occurrence of side effects from prescription drugs, and help families understand the expectations for a patient.

Common Core State Standards

This unit addresses the following Common Core State Standards:

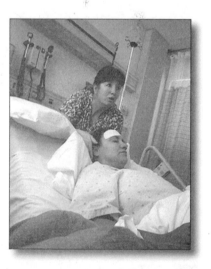

- CCSS.Math.Content.7.RP.A.1
- CCSS.Math.Content.7.RP.A.3
- CCSS.Math.Content.7.SP.B.3
- CCSS.Math.Content.7.SP.B.4
- CCSS.Math.Content.7.SP.C.5
- CCSS.Math.Content.7.SP.C.8.C

Prerequisite Skills

Prior to completing this unit, students should be proficient in the following mathematical skills: (Note: A practice sheet has been provided for each skill listed.)

- Converting between units of measure
- Describing the likelihood of an event
- Calculating the mean absolute deviation (MAD) for a data set

Name: _____   Date: _____

Unit 8: The Mathematics of Nursing

Prerequisite Skill Practice—Unit Conversions

Directions: Look up the conversion factors in a reference book or on the Internet and use them to complete the unit conversions. Round to the nearest hundredth if necessary. The first problem has been worked out as an example.

1. 32 feet = _____ centimeters $32 \text{ ft} \cdot \dfrac{12 \text{ in.}}{1 \text{ ft}} \cdot \dfrac{2.54 \text{cm}}{1 \text{ in.}} = 975.36 \text{ cm}$	2. 50 yards = _____ meters
3. 75 pounds = _____ kilograms	4. 180 kilograms = _____ ounces
5. 300 cups = _____ liters	6. 215 milliliters = _____ fluid ounces
7. 42 liters = _____ gallons	8. 2.5 miles = _____ kilometers

Name: _____ Date: _____

Unit 8: The Mathematics of Nursing

Prerequisite Skill Practice—What are the Chances?

Directions: Place an "X" on the scale above the likelihood that best describes the probability of the given situation. The first problem has been completed as an example.

1. A granite rock dropped in the water will sink.

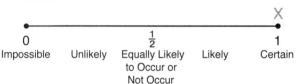

2. A 6-sided number cube will land on a 5.

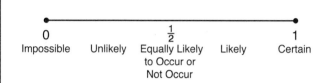

3. Tomorrow, the temperature outside will be −125°F.

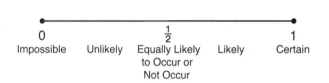

4. A vowel will be picked when a letter is randomly selected from the word *beau*.

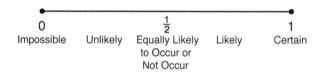

5. A red cube will be drawn when a cube is randomly selected from a bag of 100 red cubes.

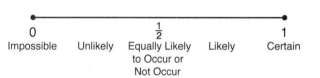

6. A vowel will be picked when a letter is randomly selected from the word *bath*.

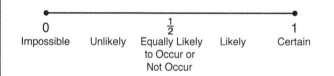

7. A flipped coin will land on heads.

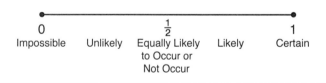

8. A flipped coin will land on heads 10 times in a row.

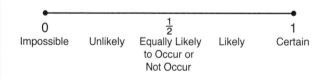

9. A red card will be picked when a card is randomly selected from a standard, 52-card deck.

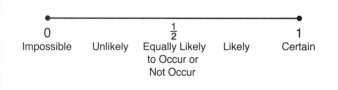

10. A number greater than 2 is drawn when randomly selecting a number from 0 – 9.

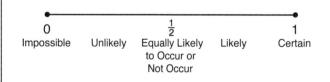

Name: _____ Date: _____

Unit 8: The Mathematics of Nursing

Prerequisite Skill Practice—Mean Absolute Deviation

Directions: For each data set, calculate the mean absolute deviation (MAD). The first problem has been worked out as an example.

1. 10, 11, 33, 41, 48, 51, 58, 59, 63, 72

Mean: 44.6

Values	Distance between the value and the mean
10	34.6
11	33.6
33	11.6
41	3.6
48	3.4
51	6.4
58	13.4
59	14.4
63	18.4
72	27.4

Mean Absolute Deviation: 16.68

2. 9, 34, 43, 57, 63, 64, 91, 94, 96, 99

3. 1.9, 3.3, 3.9, 4.0, 5.1, 6.8, 7.1, 8.2, 9.1, 9.1

4. 59, 62, 105, 125, 135, 206, 215, 221, 222, 331

Name: _____ Date: _____

Unit 8: The Mathematics of Nursing

Real-Life Application

The best nurses are compassionate and quick to respond to their patients' needs. Nurses work under a lot of pressure to ensure that medications are dosed correctly, that symptoms are addressed properly, and that patients are able to rest and recover. This work requires a lot of mathematical skill. In this unit, we will explore some of the mathematics that nurses use daily.

Converting Weights and Measures

Katie is a pediatric nurse, which means that her patients are children. Giving medications to children is especially tricky because the amount that is safe for them to receive depends on how much they weigh. One of her patients is receiving acetaminophen, which is dosed at 15 mg/kg.

1. Taria weighs 18 pounds, and Katie has to determine how much acetaminophen to give her.

a. How many kilograms does Taria weigh? _____

b. How many milligrams should Taria receive per dose? _____

c. Acetaminophen is given to children in liquid form. Liquid acetaminophen contains 160 mg per 5 mL. Set up and solve a proportion to determine how many milliliters of acetaminophen Taria should receive to get the correct amount of medication.

_____

2. Santino weighs 65 pounds. How many milliliters of acetaminophen should he receive for each dose?

_____

Name: _____ Date: _____

Unit 8: The Mathematics of Nursing

Real-Life Application (cont.)

Nurse practitioners are advanced-practice nurses who serve as primary-care providers for patients. Nurse practitioners can prescribe medications to their patients as needed.

Predicting Side Effects

Dody is a nurse practitioner, and her patient is in need of Medication A. The use of any prescription drug comes with the risk of side effects. The common potential side effects and the probability of these side effects presenting from Medication A are noted in the table below.

Side Effect	Probability
Difficulty Breathing	0.002
Drowsiness	0.08
Nausea	0.12
Skin Reaction	0.1

3. Dody is advising her patient on the use of Medication A. The patient is very concerned about the potential side effects. Help Dody by describing the likelihood of each of these side effects occurring.

_____

_____

_____

4. Dody is following up with the patients who were prescribed Medication A to determine if any have experienced side effects. If she calls 8 patients, what is the probability that she talks to at least one patient who has experienced a skin reaction as a side effect? Use this table of random digits to design a simulation to estimate this probability.

```
57455  72455  93949  03017  33463  50612  65976  18630  26080  99135
01177  18110  31846  33144  99175  43471  29341  07096  69643  85566
25107  69058  16098  53085  88020  30108  81469  33487  55936  34594
73312  70522  45206  00165  06447  65724  29908  96532  14636  25790
72526  06721  23176  95705  10722  72474  01434  38573  08089  09806
68868  49240  16140  11046  38620  49148  80338  45266  39020  06304
45101  17710  54682  31812  76734  87045  96291  67557  18680  18886
12672  99918  24766  14132  63739  18576  80955  67381  60403  09892
12201  94684  41296  86044  83170  95446  14032  86602  34998  49065
46062  88535  71445  10422  72088  50200  55509  03741  73748  38899
```

a. How will you represent the outcome of experiencing a skin reaction as a side effect?

_____

_____

_____

Name: _____ Date: _____

Unit 8: The Mathematics of Nursing

Real-Life Application (cont.)

b. What constitutes a trial for this scenario?

_____

_____

_____

c. What constitutes a success in a trial for this scenario?

_____

_____

_____

d. Execute 20 trials and list your results.

e. Based on your simulation, what is the probability that at least one of the eight patients Dody calls will have experienced a skin reaction?

_____

_____

_____

_____

Name: _____ Date: _____

Unit 8: The Mathematics of Nursing

Real-Life Application (cont.)

Average Hospital Stays

      Lorenzo is a nurse in the cardiovascular unit at the hospital. He cares for patients who have had open-heart surgery. Patients generally stay in the hospital for anywhere from 4 to 26 days to recover. To provide his patients with the best possible care, it is important for Lorenzo to understand about how long patients need to stay in the hospital.

      Below are two dot plots that represent the length of hospital stays of 15 women and 15 men after surgery.

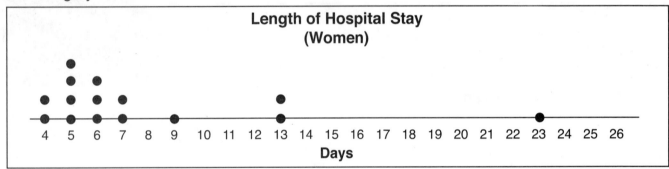

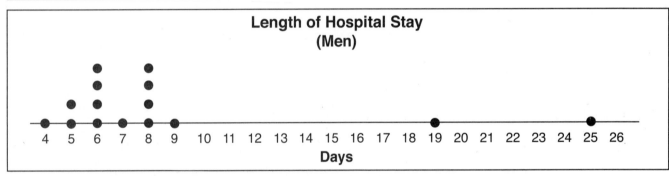

5.) By looking at the dot plots, do men or women appear to stay longer in the hospital after an open-heart surgery? Explain your reasoning.

_____

_____

_____

6.) By looking at the dot plots, do men or women appear to have the greater variability in the length of stay after an open-heart surgery?

_____

_____

_____

Name: _____ Date: _____

Unit 8: The Mathematics of Nursing

Real-Life Application (cont.)

7. What are the mean and the mean absolute deviation (MAD) for the women?

_____

8. What are the mean and the mean absolute deviation (MAD) for the men?

_____

9. Do the means and the mean absolute deviations calculated in #7 and #8 support your answers to #5 and #6?

_____

_____

_____

_____

_____

10. Suppose Lorenzo is talking with a family about a patient's recovery after surgery. How long should he tell the family to expect the patient to be in the hospital?

_____

_____

_____

Name: _____ Date: _____

Unit 9: The Mathematics of Accounting

Introduction

Accountants use mathematics for nearly every aspect of their jobs, and much of the mathematics used is found in a typical middle-school curriculum. Whether distributing corporate assets, filing tax returns, or balancing a budget, accountants use basic arithmetic and algebra skills to complete many of their daily tasks. By completing calculations such as addition, subtraction, multiplication, and division of positive and negative integers, fractions, decimals, and percents, accountants can earn a median salary of $63,550.

In the business world, accountants may be responsible for providing input when companies create budgets. They might need to determine percentages or dollar amounts of available funds to be allocated to the various divisions within a company. Doing so requires excellent command of the skills necessary to work with percents and money.

Tax accountants help people and corporations file taxes with various levels of government in the most advantageous way possible while adhering to all applicable laws and regulations. Being able to use simple formulas, compare numerical values, and add or subtract dollar amounts are important aspects of filing taxes.

Accountants also spend time balancing budgets by tracking income and expenses to be sure no more money is spent than is available. Maintaining a balanced budget requires the ability to keep detailed financial records, work with positive and negative values, and predict future financial scenarios based on past practices and current trends. Each of these areas requires a certain degree of mastery of mathematical skills in order to be handled appropriately.

These are just a few of the ways accountants use mathematics and will be the focus of this unit as students explore some of the math used in the field of accounting.

Common Core State Standards

This unit addresses the following Common Core State Standards:

- CCSS.Math.Content.7.RP.A.3
- CCSS.Math.Content.7.NS.A.1
- CCSS.Math.Content.7.NS.A.3
- CCSS.Math.Content.7.EE.B.3
- CCSS.Math.Content.7.EE.B.4

Prerequisite Skills

Prior to completing this unit, students should be proficient in the following mathematical skills: (Note: A practice sheet has been provided for each skill listed.)

- Calculating values involving fractions
- Calculating values involving percents
- Solving basic linear equations and inequalities

Name: _____   Date: _____

Unit 9: The Mathematics of Accounting

Prerequisite Skill Practice—Fractions

Directions: Complete each exercise as indicated. Show your work. The first problem has been worked out as an example.

1. What is $\frac{3}{4}$ of $\frac{2}{5}$ of $\frac{1}{8}$? $\frac{3}{\overset{}{\underset{2}{4}}} \cdot \frac{\overset{1}{2}}{5} \cdot \frac{1}{8} = \frac{3}{80}$	2. A group of 6 friends work together to build 30 birdhouses. The birdhouses sell for a total of $720, and the friends split the earnings equally. How much money does each friend receive?
3. A company allocates $\frac{1}{4}$ of its $822,000 budget to its marketing division. If $\frac{1}{6}$ of the marketing funds go toward radio advertising, how much money is spent on radio advertising?	4. What fraction of 855 is 135?
5. A woman withdraws $642 from her bank account, leaving her with $\frac{17}{20}$ of her initial balance. How much was in the woman's bank account prior to the withdrawal?	6. Simplify completely: $\frac{6}{25} \div \frac{16}{15}$
7. Simplify completely and write the result as a mixed number: $\frac{4}{5} \div \frac{8}{15} - \frac{1}{2} \cdot \frac{3}{4}$	8. What fraction of his $1,800 savings would a boy spend on a new bicycle that costs $510?

Name: _____ Date: _____

Unit 9: The Mathematics of Accounting

Prerequisite Skill Practice—Percents

Directions: Complete each exercise as indicated. Show your work. The first problem has been worked out as an example.

1. A dress originally costing $75 goes on sale for $40. To the nearest tenth, what is the percent decrease in price? Amount of decrease: $75 − $40 = $35 Percent decrease: $\frac{35}{75} = 0.4\overline{6} \approx 0.467 = 46.7\%$ The decrease in price is about 46.7%.	2. Calculate the total cost of an item marked $349.99 after 7% sales tax.
3. The payroll department of a company was originally allocated 40% of the company's total budget. However, the company re-evaluated and allocated 30% more money than originally planned. What percent of the company's total budget now goes to payroll?	4. A company decreased the amount of funding for its marketing department from 28% to 25% of the company's total budget. To the nearest tenth of a percent, determine the percent decrease in funding for the marketing department.
5. What percent of 640 is 208?	6. What is 35% of 72% of 380?
7. A man's gross income (the amount before tax) was $72,546.93 last year. After taxes, his net income was $51,798.51. To the nearest tenth, what percent of his gross income did the man pay in taxes?	8. $27,540 is 85% of what dollar amount?

Name: _____ Date: _____

Unit 9: The Mathematics of Accounting

Prerequisite Skill Practice—Linear Equations and Inequalities

Directions: Complete each exercise as indicated. Show your work. The first problem has been worked out as an example.

1. Solve the following equation: $$9x - 4 = 71$$ $9x - \cancel{4} = 71$ $\underline{+\cancel{4} \quad + 4}$ $\dfrac{9x}{9} = \dfrac{75}{9}$ $x = \dfrac{25}{3}$	**2.** Roberto currently has $350 in his savings account. Write an equation for the total amount, *A*, in his savings account after *m* months if he deposits $40 per month into the account.
3. Solve the following inequality: $$12(x + 11) > 8$$	**4.** A salesman is paid $400 per week plus 8% commission on the merchandise he sells. Write an inequality to determine the value of merchandise, *m*, the salesman must sell in order to earn at least $1,000 in one week.
5. A woman decides to recycle a number of old appliances. The recycling center will accept the first 3 appliances for free, but each additional appliance costs the owner $15 to recycle. Write an equation to determine how many appliances the woman recycled if she was charged $120.	**6.** Solve the following equation: $$\frac{3}{4}(x + 22) = \frac{1}{2}$$

Name: _____ Date: _____

Unit 9: The Mathematics of Accounting

Real-Life Application

Although advanced mathematics is not commonly encountered in accounting, accountants possess a solid mastery of basic arithmetic and algebra skills along with the ability to pay keen attention to detail. This unit explores some of the mathematics used by accountants as they perform extremely critical financial tasks.

Allocating Funds

1. An accountant is tasked with tracking the manner in which funds have been allocated to various divisions within a company. Of particular interest to the company's executive board is the level of funding provided to the Research and Development division (R&D). To promote technological innovation this year, the board increases the share of the company's total budget allocated to R&D by 15% over its previous share.

a. R&D was funded by 9.6% of the company's total budget last year. What percent of the company's total budget is allocated to R&D this year?

_____

_____

b. As a result of numerous corporate successes, the company's total budget increased by 25% this year compared to last year. What is the associated percent increase in the dollar amount provided to R&D this year? Use mathematics to support your answer.

_____

_____

Name: _____ Date: _____

Unit 9: The Mathematics of Accounting

Real-Life Application (cont.)

Operating Costs and Income

2. A small business has three employees receiving equal pay and benefits. Each employee earns $4,622.55 per month and has a benefit package costing $478.52 per month. This month, the business spent $14,562.83 on materials and supplies, $7,551.24 on rent and utilities, and $3,090.92 on all other miscellaneous costs combined. Assuming there are no other costs associated with running the business, how much revenue must the business generate this month to break even? Explain your reasoning.

_____

_____

3. A company has a total of $500,000 budgeted for payroll, marketing, and quality control. The payroll department of the company spends four times as much as the marketing department, which spends $11,000 per month more than the quality control department. If quality control spends $7,500 per month, how many months will the company be able to operate all three departments before its budget is depleted?

_____

_____

Name: _____ Date: _____

Unit 9: The Mathematics of Accounting

Real-Life Application (cont.)

 4. An accountant assists a client in preparing her state income tax form. The client's gross income for the tax year was $58,427.90, and she inherited $25,000.00 from her deceased grandfather through his will. How much does the client owe the state in taxes if personal income and inheritance are taxed at rates of 3.07% and 4.5%, respectively?

_____

_____

5. AlgebraTech is a company that was founded by four friends who each own equal shares of the business. TrigCorp recently invested in AlgebraTech such that TrigCorp now owns two-fifths of AlgebraTech. What percent of AlgebraTech does each of its founders own after Trig-Corp's investment? Support your answer using mathematics.

_____

_____

Name: _____   Date: _____

Unit 9: The Mathematics of Accounting

Real-Life Application (cont.)

6. An accountant studies a company's net income over the past five years. He notes the following changes in net income, where each value is in comparison to the net income from the previous year:

Year 1: increase of 30%   Year 2: increase of 40%
Year 3: decrease of 15%   Year 4: increase of 25%
Year 5: decrease of 10%

To the nearest hundredth of a percent, what is the percent change in the company's net income since the beginning of the study? Use mathematics to justify your answer.

_____

_____

7. A nonprofit organization paid $15,506.21 for new office furniture. During a regular review of monthly purchases, the organization's corporate accountant noticed that they were charged 6% sales tax when billed for the furniture. However, nonprofit organizations are exempt from sales tax, so no tax should have been paid. By how much did the organization overpay due to being charged sales tax on the furniture purchase?

_____

_____

Name: _____ Date: _____

Unit 9: The Mathematics of Accounting

Real-Life Application (cont.)

Budgeting for a New Product

8. A company currently budgets $94,500 to manufacture items sold to consumers. The company wants to know if it would be profitable to manufacture a particular new product. A study revealed that the company would need to manufacture 1,000 of the new items to meet market demands. The manufacturing process to produce 1,000 items would cost the company $720, and the raw materials to create each item cost $6.84.

a. What percent of the available budget must be used to manufacture 1,000 items of the new product?

_____

_____

b. To be profitable enough for the company to move forward with manufacturing the new product, sales of the product must generate revenue equal to twice the production costs; that is, the company will only make and sell the new product if a 100% profit can be realized. Assuming all 1,000 items are sold, what is the minimum unit price that would need to be charged per item in order for the new product to be profitable enough for the company to proceed with plans to bring it to market?

_____

_____

Answer Keys

Unit 1: Lawn Care
Two-Step Inequalities (p. 3)

2) $\quad 5 \le 11 + 3x$
$\quad\quad -6 \le 3x$
$\quad\quad -2 \le x$

3) $\quad 2x - 7 < -5$
$\quad\quad 2x < 2$
$\quad\quad\quad x < 1$

4) $\quad -18 \le -7x - 4$
$\quad\quad -14 \le -7x$
$\quad\quad\quad 2 \ge x$

5) $\quad -5x + 1 < 1$
$\quad\quad -5x < 0$
$\quad\quad\quad x > 0$

6) $\quad -15 \ge 4x + 3$
$\quad\quad -18 \ge 4x$
$\quad\quad -4\frac{1}{2} \ge x$

7) $\quad -7 \ge -3 + \frac{1}{5}x$
$\quad\quad -4 \ge \frac{1}{5}x$
$\quad\quad -20 \ge x$

8) $\quad -2 - \frac{2}{3}x \ge 6$
$\quad\quad -\frac{2}{3}x \ge 8$
$\quad\quad\quad x \le -12$

Integer Subtraction (p. 4)

2) $-10 - 19 = -10 + (-19) = -|10 + 19| = -29$

3) $-23 - (-15) = -23 + 15 = -|23 - 15| = -8$

4) $34 - 90 = 34 + (-90) = -|90 - 34| = -56$

5) $-28 - 34 = -28 + -34 = -|28 + 34| = -62$

6) $44 - (-7) = 44 + 7 = 51$

7) $12 - 59 = 12 + (-59) = -|59 - 12| = -47$

8) $-17 - (-52) = -17 + 52 = |52 - 17| = 35$

Area of Composite Figures (p. 5)

2) $14 \cdot 6 + \frac{1}{2} \cdot 8 \cdot 6 = 84 + 24 = 108 \text{ ft}^2$

3) $21 \cdot 16 + \frac{1}{2} \cdot 21 \cdot 3 = 336 + 31.5 = 367.5 \text{ in.}^2$

4) $35 \cdot 10 + \frac{1}{2}\pi(10.5^2) = 350 + 173.18 = 523.18 \text{ cm}^2$

5) $\frac{1}{2} \cdot 11 \cdot 11 + \frac{1}{2} \cdot \pi \cdot (7.8^2) = 60.5 + 95.6 = 156.17 \text{ in.}^2$

6) $2.5 \cdot 2.5 + \frac{3}{4} \cdot \pi + (2.5^2) = 6.25 + 14.73 = 20.98 \text{ ft}^2$

The Mathematics of Lawn Care (p. 6–9)

1) $24.97 \cdot 5 = 124.85$
$179.95 + 89.95 + 124.85 + 20.95 = \$415.70$

2) $35m - 415.70 \ge 450$
$\quad\quad 35m \ge 865.70$
$\quad\quad\quad m \ge 24.73$
Oscar needs to mow at least 25 lawns to make enough money for his trumpet.

3) $35m - 215.70 \ge 450$
$\quad\quad 35m \ge 665.70$
$\quad\quad\quad m \ge 19.02$
Oscar needs to mow at least 20 lawns to make enough money for his trumpet.

4) $35m - 290.70 \ge 450$
$\quad\quad 35m \ge 740.70$
$\quad\quad\quad m \ge 21.16$
Oscar needs to mow at least 22 lawns to make enough money for his trumpet.

5)
 a) $8 \cdot 11 + 16 \cdot 30 = 88 + 480 = 568 \text{ ft}^2$
 b) $568 \div 150 = 3.79$ hours
 c) $3.79 \cdot 12.50 = \$47.38$

6) $2(8)(24) + \frac{1}{2}(\pi)(13^2) = 384 + 265.46 = 649.46 \text{ ft}^2$
$649.46 \div 150 = 4.33$ hours
$4.33 \cdot 12.50 = \$54.13$

7)
 a) House A is 9 units from Kendra's house.
 b) House C is 3 units from Kendra's house.
 c) House A is 12 units from House C.
 d) $9 - (-3)$
 e) The distance between house A and house C is the absolute value of their difference.
 $\quad |9 - (-3)| = |-3 - 9| = 12$

8) The distance from Kendra's house to house A is 9, and the distance from Kendra's house to house D is 16. I can find the distance between the two houses by finding the absolute value of their difference.
$|16 - 9| = |9 - 16| = 7$

9) $|-16 - (-12)| = |-16 + 12| = |-4| = 4$
The distance from house E to house B is 4 units.

Unit 2: Yard Sales

Multiplying Rational Numbers (p. 11)

2) $\frac{7}{9} \cdot 245.7 = \frac{7}{9} \cdot \frac{245.7}{1} = \frac{1719.9}{9} = 191.1$

3) $\frac{5}{7} \cdot \frac{14}{17} = \frac{70}{119} = \frac{10}{17}$

4) $\frac{9}{11} \cdot \frac{5}{6} = \frac{45}{66} = \frac{15}{22}$

5) $2.33 \cdot 15.194 = 35.40202$

6) $0.87 \cdot 9.1 = 7.917$

7) $4.5 \cdot \frac{13}{15} = \frac{4.5}{1} \cdot \frac{13}{15} = \frac{58.5}{15} = 3.9$

8) $19 \cdot 123.76 = 2{,}351.44$

Writing and Solving Equations (p. 12)

2) Let *b* represent Bentley's weight and *d* represent Daphne's weight. Then $b = \frac{2}{3}d$.

Since $d = 72$, $b = \frac{2}{3} \cdot 72$ or 48.
Bentley weighs 48 pounds.

3) Let *w* represent the length of a great white shark and *m* represent the man's height. Then $w = 4m$. Since $m = 1.6$, $w = 4 \cdot 1.6$ or 6.4. The great white shark is 6.4 meters long.

4) Let *t* represent Octavia's sales today and *y* represent Octavia's sales yesterday.
Then $t = 0.72y$. Since $y = \$635.90$,
$t = 0.72 \cdot 635.90$ or 457.848.
Octavia's sales today were about $457.85.

5) Let *n* represent Wing's desired weight and *c* represent Wing's weight.
Then $n = c + 0.12c$ or $n = 1.12c$.
Since $c = 108$, $n = 1.12 \cdot 108$ or 120.96.
Wing needs to weigh about 121 pounds.

6) Let *s* represent the sale price of the jeans and *p* represent the original price of the jeans.
Then $s = p - 0.30p$ or $s = 0.70p$.
Since $p = \$42.60$, $s = 0.70 \cdot 42.60$ or 29.82.
The sale price of the jeans is $29.82.

7) Let *a* represent the amount that Sandra will have left in her account and *b* represent the amount she earned when she sold her bicycle.

Then $a = 210.15 - \frac{1}{4}b$.

Since $b = 124$, $a = 210.15 - \left(\frac{1}{4} \cdot 124\right)$

or 179.15. Sandra will have $179.15 left in her account.

8) Let *c* represent the number of tickets Colton sold and *x* represent the number of tickets Xavier sold to his family.
Then $c = 89 + 1.2x$.
Since $x = 30$, $c = 89 + (1.2 \cdot 30)$ or 125.
Colton sold 125 tickets.

Understanding Probability (p. 13)

2) Likely; probability is closer to 1 than 0

3) Neither likely nor unlikely; probability is $\frac{1}{2}$

4) Likely; probability is closer to 1 than 0

5) Neither likely nor unlikely; probability is $\frac{1}{2}$

6) Neither likely nor unlikely; probability is close to $\frac{1}{2}$

7) Unlikely; probability is closer to 0 than 1

8) Unlikely; probability is closer to 0 than 1

The Mathematics of Yard Sales (p. 14–18)

1)
a) *Sample answer:* Let *s* represent the number of friends who suggest Saturday and *f* represent the number of friends who suggest Friday. Then $s = 4f$.

b) $s = 4f = 4 \cdot 6 = 24$; Twenty-four friends recommended that you hold your yard sale on Saturday.

c) Six friends suggested Friday and 24 friends suggested Saturday. So a total of 30 friends suggested the yard sale should be on Friday or Saturday.

2)
a) $d = c - 0.18c$
b) $d = 0.82c$
c) *Sample answer:* The equations will yield the same results.
d) $d = 0.82c = 0.82 \cdot 5.97 = 4.8954$; The cost of one sign is $4.90. So the cost of 8 signs is $8 \cdot 4.90$ or $39.20.

3)
a) Let *s* represent the selling price and *p* represent the original price.

Then $s = \frac{1}{3}p$.

b) Let *s* represent the selling price and *p* represent the original price.
Then $s = 0.10p$.

c)

Item	Recommended Yard Sale Price
Lamp	$14.26
Glass pitcher	$4.32
Frame	$3.30
Toaster	$16.65
Chainsaw	$16.48

d)

Item	Actual Yard Sale Price
Lamp	$14.25
Glass pitcher	$4.25
Frame	$3.25
Toaster	$16.75
Chainsaw	$16.50

4)

a) *Sample answer:* No, the probabilities are not equally likely, because the areas that represent the different discounts are different sizes.

b) The spinner is most likely to land on 10% off because that is the biggest section on the spinner.

c) The spinner is least likely to land on 60% off because that is the smallest section on the spinner.

d) The spinner is likely to land on 20% off $\frac{1}{4}$ of the time because that section is $\frac{1}{4}$ of the circle.

5) *Sample answer:* The spinner should be divided into 6 equally sized sections and each section should be marked with a discount of 10%, 20%, etc. Students could also choose to divide the spinner into 12 equally sized sections and mark two sections with each of the discount amounts.

6)

a) *Sample answer:* Yes, all of the discounts are equally likely with this model because the probability of rolling each of the numbers is equally likely.

b) *Sample answer:* It will yield the same results as the model in #5. But it is an easier model because you don't have to measure angles and create it.

Unit 3: Food Pantries

Ratios and Proportions (p. 20)

2) $\frac{32}{t} = \frac{9}{20} \longrightarrow 640 = 9t \longrightarrow t = 640 \div 9 \longrightarrow$ $t = \frac{640}{9}$ or $t = 71\frac{1}{9}$

3) $167 \div 4 = \frac{167}{4}$ or $41\frac{3}{4}$ or 41.75; The motorcycle travels 41.75 miles per gallon.

4) $\frac{r}{15} = \frac{40}{21} \longrightarrow 21r = 600 \longrightarrow r = 600 \div 21$ $\longrightarrow r = \frac{200}{7}$ or $r = 28\frac{4}{7}$

5) $\frac{3}{8} = \frac{k}{10} \longrightarrow 30 = 8k \longrightarrow k = 30 \div 8 \longrightarrow$ $k = \frac{15}{4}$ or $k = 3\frac{3}{4}$ or $k = 3.75$

6) $\frac{7}{4} = \frac{518}{x} \longrightarrow 7x = 2,072 \longrightarrow$ $x = 2,072 \div 7 \longrightarrow x = 296;$ There are 296 cans of vegetables.

7) $\frac{14}{85} = \frac{98}{d} \longrightarrow 14d = 8,330 \longrightarrow$ $d = 8,330 \div 14 \longrightarrow d = 595$

8) $4.65 \cdot 2.79 = 12.9735;$ The grapes cost $12.97.

Algebraic Equations and Inequalities (p. 21)

2) $A = 14.95m + 25.00$ or $A = 25.00 + 14.95m$

3) $382 + 60b \geq 1,000$ or $60b + 382 \geq 1000$

4) $0.8x - 3.9 = 5.3 \longrightarrow$ $0.8x - 3.9 + 3.9 = 5.3 + 3.9 \longrightarrow$ $0.8x = 9.2 \longrightarrow x = 9.2 \div 0.8 \longrightarrow x = 11.5$

5) $7x + 24 \leq 59 \longrightarrow 7x + 24 - 24 \leq 59 - 24$ $\longrightarrow 7x \leq 35 \longrightarrow x \leq 35 \div 7 \longrightarrow x \leq 5$

6) $40 + 15.5c \leq 96$ or $15.5c + 40 \leq 96$

7) $-\frac{2}{5}\left(x + \frac{1}{4}\right) = \frac{7}{10} \longrightarrow x + \frac{1}{4} = \frac{7}{\overset{1}{\cancel{10}}} \cdot \left(-\frac{\cancel{5}}{2}\right)$ $\longrightarrow x + \frac{1}{4} = -\frac{7}{4} \longrightarrow x = -\frac{7}{4} - \frac{1}{4} \longrightarrow$ $x = -\frac{8}{4} \longrightarrow x = -2$

8) $\frac{2}{3}\left(x - 5\frac{1}{4}\right) = 6\frac{7}{8} \longrightarrow \frac{2}{3}\left(x - \frac{21}{4}\right) = \frac{55}{8} \longrightarrow$ $x - \frac{21}{4} = \frac{165}{16} \longrightarrow x = \frac{165}{16} + \frac{84}{16} \longrightarrow$ $x = \frac{249}{16}$ or $x = 15\frac{9}{16}$

Perimeter, Area, and Volume (p. 22)

2) Area of each face of cube:

$$A = s^2 = \left(2\frac{3}{4}\right)^2 = \left(\frac{11}{4}\right)^2 = \frac{11^2}{4^2} = \frac{121}{16}$$

Total surface area of cube (6 faces):

$$SA = 6A = 6\left(\frac{121}{16}\right) = \frac{\overset{3}{\cancel{6}}}{1} \cdot \frac{121}{\underset{8}{\cancel{16}}} = \frac{363}{8}$$

or $45\frac{3}{8}$

The cube has a surface area of $45\frac{3}{8}$ in^2.

3) $A = \frac{1}{2}bh \longrightarrow 60 = \frac{1}{2}(8)h \longrightarrow$

$$60 = \underset{1}{\frac{1}{\cancel{2}}} \cdot \frac{\overset{4}{\cancel{8}}}{1} \cdot h \longrightarrow 60 = 4h \longrightarrow$$

$h = 60 \div 4 \longrightarrow h = 15$

The triangle has a height of 15 ft.

4) $V = Bh = 6.28(14.75) = 92.63$ m^3.

5) Area of square base: $A = s^2 = 3^2 = 9$;
perimeter of square base: $p = 4s = 4(3) = 12$
Surface area of prism: $SA = 2A + ph =$
$2(9) + 12(5) = 18 + 60 = 78$ ft^2

6) $C = 2\pi r = 2\pi(48) = 96\pi$ mm

7) $C = 2.8\pi \longrightarrow 2\pi r = 2.8\pi \longrightarrow$

$$r = \frac{2.8\cancel{\pi}}{2\cancel{\pi}} \longrightarrow r = \frac{2.8}{2} \longrightarrow r = 1.4$$
$A = \pi r^2 = \pi(1.4)^2 = \pi(1.96) = 1.96\pi$ in.^{2}

8) $V = lwh = (28.4)(22)(9.8) = 6{,}123.04$ cm^3

The Mathematics of Food Pantries (p. 23–26)

1)
   a) $65{,}982.00 \div 9{,}426 = 7$;
   The unit price is $7.00 per pound.
   b) $140{,}000 \cdot 7.00 = 980{,}000$;
   Helping Hands needs to budget $980,000 for next year.

2)
   a) $3{,}680 + 35b = 5{,}245$ or
   $35b + 3{,}680 = 5{,}245$
   b) $3{,}680 + 35b \longrightarrow 35b = 5{,}245 - 3{,}680$
   $\longrightarrow 35b = 1{,}565 \longrightarrow 1{,}565 \div 35 \longrightarrow$

   $b = 44\frac{5}{7}$
   Since you cannot have a partial business sponsor, you need to round up to be sure there is enough to cover the budget, so Helping Hands needs 45 local business sponsors.

3) $126{,}582 \cdot 0.1422 = 17{,}999.9604$;
Since there cannot be part of a household, round the result to get 18,000 households in the region that require food assistance.

4) You need to multiply the number of households in need by the number of people in each household by the number of pounds of food per person by the number of days.
$18{,}000 \cdot 3.5 \cdot 4 \cdot 7 = 1{,}764{,}000$;
Helping Hands should plan to distribute 1,764,000 pounds of food to help every person in the region avoid going hungry.
Sample answer: The full amount of food may not need to be distributed each week because some households may only need a small amount of food to supplement what they are able to afford on their own, some people may not need food every week but rather only the last few days before their next paycheck arrives, some people may find a job and stop needing food assistance altogether, etc.

5) Note that the height of the boxes is irrelevant for calculating the number of boxes to be stored in the warehouse as a specific number of boxes to be in each stack is provided.
Number of boxes along length:

$$70 \div 1\frac{3}{4} = \frac{\overset{10}{\cancel{70}}}{1} \cdot \frac{4}{\underset{1}{\cancel{7}}} = 40;$$

or b) $70 \div 1\frac{1}{4} = \frac{\overset{14}{\cancel{70}}}{1} \cdot \frac{4}{\underset{1}{\cancel{5}}} = 56$

Number of boxes along width:

$$35 \div 1\frac{1}{4} = \frac{\overset{7}{\cancel{35}}}{1} \cdot \frac{4}{\underset{1}{\cancel{5}}} = 28$$

or b) $35 \div 1\frac{3}{4} = \frac{\overset{5}{\cancel{35}}}{1} \cdot \frac{4}{\underset{1}{\cancel{7}}} = 20$

Number of boxes in one layer on the floor:
$40 \cdot 28 = 1{,}120$ or b) $56 \cdot 20 = 1{,}120$
Total number of boxes in all layers:
$1{,}120 \cdot 6 = 6{,}720$
Helping Hands Food Pantry can store 6,720 boxes in the warehouse.

6) Area of delivery region: $A = \pi r^2 = \pi(6)^2 = \pi(36) = 36\pi \approx 36 \cdot 3.14 \approx 113.04$
Number of drivers needed:
$113.04 \div 30 = 3.768$
Since you cannot have part of a driver, you need to round up, so Helping Hands needs 4 drivers to continue the delivery service.

7)

    a) $96 + 3n > 150$ or $3n + 96 > 150$

    b) $96 + 3n > 150 \longrightarrow$
       $\cancel{96} + 3n - \cancel{96} > 150 - 96 \longrightarrow$
       $3n > 54 \longrightarrow 54 \div 3 \longrightarrow n > 18$
       Since the goal is to devote more than 150 hours to distributing food, at least 19 volunteer shifts need to be filled.
       Sample answer: This does not necessarily mean that 19 volunteers are needed. It is possible for one volunteer to work multiple shifts, requiring less than 19 volunteers. Or there may be a need for multiple volunteers to work each shift, requiring more than 19 volunteers.

Unit 4: Mechanics
Evaluating Expressions (p. 28)

2) $a = -\frac{2}{9}b + 13 \longrightarrow a = -\frac{2}{9}(-27) + 13 \longrightarrow$
$a = -\frac{2}{9}\left(\frac{-27}{1}\right) + 13 \longrightarrow a = \frac{54}{9} + 13 \longrightarrow$
$a = 6 + 13 \longrightarrow a = 19$

3) $r = \frac{5}{8}s - 23 \longrightarrow r = \frac{5}{8}(-64) - 23 \longrightarrow$
$r = \frac{5}{8}\left(\frac{-64}{1}\right) - 23 \longrightarrow r = \frac{-320}{8} - 23 \longrightarrow$
$r = -40 - 23 \longrightarrow r = -63$

4) $m = -\frac{5}{6}n - 19 \longrightarrow m = -\frac{5}{6}(-42) - 19$
$\longrightarrow m = -\frac{5}{6}\left(\frac{-42}{1}\right) - 19 \longrightarrow m = \frac{210}{6} - 19$
$\longrightarrow m = 35 - 19 \longrightarrow m = 16$

5) $w = \frac{7}{8}x + 21 \longrightarrow w = \frac{7}{8}(32) + 21 \longrightarrow$
$w = \frac{7}{8}\left(\frac{32}{1}\right) + 21 \longrightarrow w + \frac{224}{8} + 21 \longrightarrow$
$w = 28 + 21 \longrightarrow w = 49$

6) $p = -\frac{5}{9}r + 17 \longrightarrow p = -\frac{5}{9}(18) + 17 \longrightarrow$
$p = -\frac{5}{9}\left(\frac{18}{1}\right) + 17 \longrightarrow p = -\frac{90}{9} + 17 \longrightarrow$
$p = -10 + 17 \longrightarrow p = 7$

7) $k = \frac{2}{3}l - 35 \longrightarrow k = \frac{2}{3}(33) - 35 \longrightarrow$
$k = \frac{2}{3}\left(\frac{33}{1}\right) - 35 \longrightarrow k = \frac{66}{3} - 35 \longrightarrow$
$k = 22 - 35 \longrightarrow k = -13$

8) $q = -\frac{5}{12}r - 25 \longrightarrow q = -\frac{5}{12}(36) - 25 \longrightarrow$
$q = -\frac{5}{12}\left(\frac{36}{1}\right) - 25 \longrightarrow q = -\frac{180}{12} - 25$
$\longrightarrow q = -15 - 25 \longrightarrow q = -40$

Identifying Proportional Relationships (p. 29)

2) Proportional; $\frac{5}{1} = \frac{10}{2} = \frac{15}{3} = \frac{20}{4} = \frac{25}{5}$

3) Not proportional; $\frac{1}{1} = \frac{2}{2} \neq \frac{4}{3} \neq \frac{8}{4} \neq \frac{16}{5}$

4) Proportional; $\frac{4}{1} = \frac{12}{3} = \frac{24}{6} = \frac{40}{10} = \frac{80}{20}$

5) Not proportional; $\frac{1}{2} \neq \frac{1}{4} \neq \frac{2}{6} \neq \frac{3}{8} \neq \frac{5}{10}$

6) Proportional; $\frac{\frac{1}{2}}{1} = \frac{1}{2} = \frac{\frac{3}{2}}{3} = \frac{2}{4} = \frac{\frac{5}{2}}{5}$

Solving and Graphing Inequalities (p. 30)

2) $2m + 7 > -3 \longrightarrow 2m + 7 - 7 > -3 - 7$
$\longrightarrow \frac{2m}{2} > \frac{-10}{2} \longrightarrow m > -5$

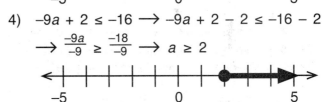

3) $-5b + 8 < 3 \longrightarrow -5b + 8 - 8 < 3 - 8$
$\longrightarrow \frac{-5b}{-5} > \frac{-5}{-5} \longrightarrow b > 1$

4) $-9a + 2 \leq -16 \longrightarrow -9a + 2 - 2 \leq -16 - 2$
$\longrightarrow \frac{-9a}{-9} \geq \frac{-18}{-9} \longrightarrow a \geq 2$

5) $-7p - 13 \geq -20 \longrightarrow$
$-7p - 13 + 13 \geq -20 + 13 \longrightarrow$
$\frac{-7p}{-7} \leq \frac{-7}{-7} \longrightarrow p \leq 1$

6) $4s - 7 < 5 \longrightarrow 4s - 7 + 7 < 5 + 7 \longrightarrow$
$\frac{4s}{4} < \frac{12}{4} \longrightarrow s < 3$

The Mathematics of Mechanics (p. 31–35)

1)

Liquid	Freezing Point (°F)	Boiling Point (°F)
Water	32	212
50/50 mix antifreeze/ water	–34.6	222.8
70/30 mix antifreeze/ water	–67	235.4

2)

a) Let *a* represent the number of quarts of antifreeze needed for the solution. Then

$\frac{a}{14} = \frac{70}{100} \rightarrow 100a = 70 \cdot 14 \rightarrow$

$\frac{100a}{100} = \frac{980}{100} \rightarrow a = 9.8$. So 9.8 quarts of antifreeze are needed.

b) Let *a* represent the number of quarts of antifreeze needed for the solution and *c* represent the capacity of the cooling system. Then the equation $\frac{a}{c} = \frac{70}{100}$ or $a = 0.7 \cdot c$ could be used to determine the number of quarts of antifreeze needed.

c) The constant of proportionality is $\frac{70}{100}$ or 0.7. This represents the ratio of the amount of antifreeze to the capacity of the cooling system because the solution needs to contain 70% antifreeze.

d) Let *w* represent the number of quarts of water needed for the solution. Then

$\frac{w}{14} = \frac{30}{100} \rightarrow 100w = 30 \cdot 14 \rightarrow$

$\frac{100w}{100} = \frac{420}{100} \rightarrow w = 4.2$. So 4.2 quarts of water are needed.

e) Let *w* represent the number of quarts of water needed for the solution and *c* represent the capacity of the cooling system. Then the equation $\frac{w}{c} = \frac{30}{100}$ or $w = 0.3 \cdot c$ could be used to determine the number of quarts of water needed.

f) The constant of proportionality is $\frac{30}{100}$ or 0.3. This represents the ratio of the amount of water to the capacity of the

cooling system because the solution needs to contain 30% water.

3)

a) The capacity of the cooling system and freezing point are not in a proportional relationship because the ratios of the freezing point to their corresponding capacities are not constant.

That is $\frac{-34}{10} \neq \frac{-23}{11} \neq \frac{-15}{12}$, etc.

b) **Capacity versus Freezing Point**

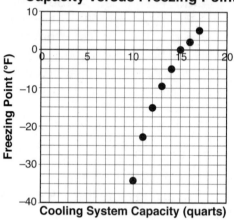

Cooling System Capacity (quarts)

c) The points on the graph are not organized in a straight line. This means that the quantities are not in a proportional relationship.

4)

a) Answers will vary.

b) **Pressure versus Boiling Point**

c) *Sample answer:* The points on the graph are organized in a straight line, which indicates that the quantities are in a proportional relationship.

d) $\dfrac{231 - 222}{3 - 0} = \dfrac{9}{3} = 3;$

$\dfrac{237 - 231}{5 - 3} = \dfrac{6}{2} = 3;$

$\dfrac{252 - 237}{10 - 5} = \dfrac{15}{5} = 3;$

$\dfrac{258 - 252}{12 - 10} = \dfrac{6}{2} = 3;$

$\dfrac{267 - 258}{15 - 12} = \dfrac{9}{3} = 3;$

$\dfrac{282 - 267}{20 - 15} = \dfrac{15}{5} = 3;$

Because the ratio is constant, I know that pressure and boiling point are in a proportional relationship.

e) See graph in 4b. The line crosses the *y*-axis at 222.

f) Let *p* represent pressure and *b* represent boiling point. Then $3p + 222 = b$.

g) $3p + 222 \le 258$

h) $3p + 222 \le 258 \longrightarrow$
$3p + 222 - 222 \le 258 - 222 \longrightarrow$
$\dfrac{3p}{3} \le \dfrac{36}{3} \longrightarrow p \le 12$

i) The solution means that any pressure that is less than or equal to 12 psi will ensure that the boiling point is at most 258°F.

Unit 5: Car Sales

Identifying Proportional Relationships (p. 37)

2) Proportional; straight line that goes through origin
3) Not proportional; not a straight line
4) Proportional; straight line that goes through origin
5) Not proportional; doesn't go through origin
6) Not proportional; not straight line and not through origin
7) Proportional; straight line that goes through origin
8) Not proportional; not a straight line

Equivalent Percent Expressions (p. 38)

2) $n + 0.10n = 1.10n$
3) $n + 0.78n = 1.78n$
4) $n - 0.14n = 0.86n$
5) $n - 0.99n = 0.01n$

6) $n + 1.50n = 2.50n$
7) $n + 0.225n = 1.225n$
8) $n - 0.01n = 0.99n$
9) $n - 0.425n = 0.575n$
10) $n + 0.0625n = 1.0625n$

Sample Spaces (p. 39)

2) H-H, H-T, T-H, T-T
3) 1-1, 1-2, 1-3, 1-4, 1-5, 1-6, 2-1, 2-2, 2-3, 2-4, 2-5, 2-6, 3-1, 3-2, 3-3, 3-4, 3-5, 3-6, 4-1, 4-2, 4-3, 4-4, 4-5, 4-6, 5-1, 5-2, 5-3, 5-4, 5-5, 5-6, 6-1, 6-2, 6-3, 6-4, 6-5, 6-6
4) R-1, R-2, R-3, R-4, R-5, B-1, B-2, B-3, B-4, B-5, Y-1, Y-2, Y-3, Y-4, Y-5, G-1, G-2, G-3, G-4, G-5
5) S-shirt, S-pants, S-socks, M-shirt, M-pants, M-socks, L-shirt, L-pants, L-socks
6) rock-rock, rock-paper, rock-scissors, paper-rock, paper-paper, paper-scissors, scissors-rock, scissors-paper, scissors-scissors

The Mathematics of Car Sales (p. 40–43)

1)
a) The relationship between the number of cold calls and the number of appointments is proportional because the points lie in a straight line that goes through the origin.

b) Point *A* shows that 500 cold calls result in 15 appointments.

c) $\dfrac{15}{500} = \dfrac{3}{100} = 0.03;$ The rate of success is 3 appointments per 100 cold calls, or 3%.

d) *Sample answer:* No, I wouldn't recommend that Chuck make cold calls. He would have to spend a lot of time making calls for very few appointments.

2)
a) The relationship between the number of referral calls and the number of appointments is proportional because the points lie in a straight line that goes through the origin.

b) Point *B* shows that 500 referral calls result in 200 appointments.

c) $\dfrac{200}{500} = \dfrac{40}{100} = 0.40;$ The rate of success is 40 appointments per 100 referral calls, or 40%.

3) $\frac{3}{100} = \frac{25}{x} \longrightarrow x = 833.\overline{3}$

Chuck would need to make 834 cold calls to get 25 appointments.

$\frac{40}{100} = \frac{25}{x} \longrightarrow x = 62.5$

Chuck would need to make 63 referral calls to get 25 appointments.

4) $\frac{18}{45} = 0.40$; The probability that a customer purchases a car is 40%.

5) $\frac{40}{100} = \frac{x}{1575} \longrightarrow 630 = x$

Chuck can expect 630 customers to purchase a car throughout the month.

6) *Sample answer:* The actual number might be different because the original data was taken on a day when there was a deal going on. Or the actual number might be different because the original data was collected on a Saturday, when there are a greater number of sales being made.

7) There are 40 different cars to select.
C-M-B, C-M-R, C-M-S, C-M-W, C-A-B, C-A-R, C-A-S, C-A-W, M-M-B, M-M-R, M-M-S, M-M-W, M-A-B, M-A-R, M-A-S, M-A-W, S-M-B, S-M-R, S-M-S, S-M-W, S-A-B, S-A-R, S-A-S, S-A-W, SUV-M-B, SUV-M-R, SUV-M-S, SUV-M-W, SUV-A-B, SUV-A-R, SUV-A-S, SUV-A-W, T-M-B, T-M-R, T-M-S, T-M-W, T-A-B, T-A-R, T-A-S, T-A-W

8) $\frac{5}{40} = 0.125$; The probability is 0.125.

9)
    a) $n + 0.07n$
    b) $1.07n$
    c) Yes, they are equivalent. Increasing the original price by 7% is the same as multiplying the original price by 1.07.
    d) $1.07(23,549) = 25,197.43$;
        Chuck would be willing to sell the vehicle for $25,197.43.

Unit 6: Marketing

Ratios, Proportions, and Scale Drawings (p. 45)

2) Area of ad: $2\frac{1}{2} \cdot 1\frac{1}{2} = \frac{5}{2} \cdot \frac{3}{2} = \frac{15}{4}$ in.²;

cost per square inch: $60 \div \frac{15}{4} = \frac{60}{1} \cdot \frac{4}{15} = 16$

The ad has a unit price of $16 per square inch.

3) $\frac{g}{35} = \frac{82}{45} \longrightarrow 45 \cdot g = 35 \cdot 82 \longrightarrow$

$45g = 2,870 \longrightarrow g = \frac{574}{9}$ or $g = 63\frac{7}{9}$ or $g = 63.\overline{7}$

4) $\frac{8}{3} = \frac{x}{471} \longrightarrow 471 \cdot 8 = 3 \cdot x \longrightarrow$
$3,768 = 3x \longrightarrow x = 1,256$
1,256 people make online purchases.

5) Number of females: $\frac{3}{4} = \frac{51}{f} \longrightarrow$
$f \cdot 3 = 4 \cdot 51 \longrightarrow 3f = 204 \longrightarrow f = 68$
Total customers: male + female =
$51 + 68 = 119$

6) Width of wall: $\frac{8 \text{ cm}}{1} \cdot \frac{3 \text{ ft}}{1 \text{ cm}} = 24$ ft;

Height of wall: $\frac{3\frac{1}{2} \text{ cm}}{1} \cdot \frac{3 \text{ ft}}{1 \text{ cm}} = \frac{7}{2} \cdot \frac{3 \text{ ft}}{1} = \frac{21}{2}$ ft

Area of wall: $A = bh = \frac{24}{1} \cdot \frac{21}{2} = 252$ ft²

7) Number of eggs: $2\frac{1}{2}$ dozen $= 2\frac{1}{2} \cdot 12 = \frac{5}{2} \cdot \frac{12}{1} = 30$
Price per egg: $4.20 \div 30 = \$0.14$

8) $\frac{7}{12} = \frac{k}{19} \longrightarrow 19 \cdot 7 = 12 \cdot k \longrightarrow$
$133 = 12k \longrightarrow k = \frac{133}{12}$ or $k = 11\frac{1}{12}$ or $k = 11.08\overline{3}$

Percents (p. 46)

2) $134\frac{7}{10} \div 56\frac{1}{8} = \frac{1347}{10} \div \frac{449}{8} =$
$\frac{1347}{10} \cdot \frac{8}{449} = \frac{12}{5} = 2.4 = 240\%$

3) Amount of decrease: $40 - 34 = 6$

Percent decrease $= \dfrac{\text{Amount of decrease}}{\text{Original estimate}} =$

$\frac{6}{40} = \frac{3}{20} = 0.15 = 15\%$

4) Tax: $89.95 \cdot 0.07 = 6.2965 \longrightarrow \$6.30$;
Total amount paid: $\$89.95 + \$6.30 = \$96.25$

5) $1,075 + 0.065x = 4,000 \longrightarrow$
$0.065x = 2,925 \longrightarrow x = 45,000$
The salesman must sell $45,000 worth of furniture to earn $4,000 for the month.

6) Amount of error: $273 - 250 = 23$

Percent error $= \dfrac{\text{Amount of error}}{\text{Original estimate}} =$

$\frac{23}{250} = 0.092 = 9.2\%$

7) $\frac{1}{5}$ of 1% of $2,750 = \frac{1}{5} \cdot \frac{1}{100} \cdot \frac{2750}{1} = \frac{11}{2}$ or $5\frac{1}{2}$ or 5.5

8) Discount: $62.55 \cdot 0.15 = 9.3825 \longrightarrow \$9.38$;
Bill after discount: $\$62.55 - \$9.38 = \$53.17$
Tax: $53.17 \cdot 0.06 = 3.1902 \longrightarrow \$3.19$;
Final amount owed: $\$53.17 + \$3.19 = \$56.36$;
The final amount due for dinner is $56.36.

Probability and Statistics (p. 47)

2) Fraction of students surveyed who like math:

$$\frac{72}{300} = \frac{6}{25}$$

Fraction of students in school who like math:

$\frac{6}{25} \cdot \frac{1492}{1} = \frac{8952}{25} = 358.08$; round to 358
Based on the survey, 358 students are expected to consider math to be their favorite subject.

3) Flipping a coin: $\frac{1}{2} = 0.5$; rolling a 3: $\frac{1}{6} = 0.1\overline{6}$;

guessing an answer: $\frac{1}{4} = 0.25$
Rolling a 3 on a number cube is the least likely event since it has the lowest probability.

4) *Sample answer:* The population being studied is average middle-class families. The average middle-class family does not own a private plane, so the sample does not represent the population.

5) *Sample answer:* The average heights of the girls and boys are 44 and 42 inches, respectively, so the difference in their mean heights is only 2 inches. The mean absolute deviation for the girls is 6 inches, meaning the shorter half of the girls are, on average, 38 inches, which is shorter than the average height of the boys. Similarly, the mean absolute deviation for the boys is 3 inches, so the taller half of the boys are, on average, 45 inches, which is taller than the average height of the girls. So although the average height of the girls is greater than that of the boys, it is not reasonable to state definitively that the girls are taller.

6) *Sample answer:* The 100 randomly sampled students represent all college students, so the results of the survey are valid, but they are only estimates and are not necessarily applicable to all specific groups of college students.

The Mathematics of Marketing (p. 48–51)

1) Area of smaller billboard: $A = bh \longrightarrow$

$10\frac{1}{2} \cdot 22\frac{1}{2} = \frac{21}{2} \cdot \frac{45}{2} = \frac{945}{4}$ ft²

Unit price of smaller billboard: $\frac{1075}{1} \div \frac{945}{4} =$

$\frac{1075}{1} \cdot \frac{4}{945} = \frac{860}{189} \approx 4.55 \longrightarrow \$4.55$ per ft²

Area of larger billboard: $A = bh \longrightarrow$
$14 \cdot 48 = 672$ ft²
Unit price of larger billboard:
$3{,}125 \div 672 \approx 4.65 \longrightarrow \$4.65$ per ft²
The smaller billboard is the better deal based on unit price per square foot.

2) $3{,}125m + 2{,}380 = 35{,}000 \longrightarrow$
$3{,}125m = 32{,}620 \longrightarrow m = 10.4384$
Since the billboard is rented by whole months, the company can rent it for 10 months.

3)

a) Chance of company's ad appearing on website's home page: $\frac{5{,}280}{200{,}000} = 0.0264$
Number of visits to website's home page in 4 weeks:
$1{,}750{,}000 \cdot 7 \cdot 4 = 49{,}000{,}000$
$49{,}000{,}000 \cdot 0.0264 = 1{,}293{,}600$; The company can expect 1,293,600 potential customers to see their banner ad.

b) *Sample answer:* People often visit websites more than once, so the number of visits to the home page is likely more than the number of individual people going to the website.

4)

a) Amount of increase:
$95{,}250 - 75{,}000 = 20{,}250$

$\text{Percent increase} = \dfrac{\text{Amount of increase}}{\text{Original amount}}$

$= \frac{20{,}250}{75{,}000} = \frac{27}{100} = 0.27 = 27\%$

b) Percent increase needed to boost sales

4%: $4 \div \frac{1}{10} = 4 \cdot 10 = 40 \longrightarrow 40\%$
Amount of increase:
$75{,}000 \cdot 0.40 = 30{,}000$
New advertising budget:
$75{,}000 + 30{,}000 = 105{,}000$
CalculoCorp would need to spend $105,000 this year to see a 4% increase in sales.

5)

a) Short leg: $7\frac{1}{2} \cdot \frac{1}{8} = \frac{15}{2} \cdot \frac{1}{8} = \frac{15}{16}$ in.

Long leg: $18 \cdot \frac{1}{8} = \frac{18}{1} \cdot \frac{1}{8} = \frac{18}{8} =$
$\frac{9}{4} = 2\frac{1}{4}$ in.

Hypotenuse: $19\frac{1}{2} \cdot \frac{1}{8} = \frac{39}{2} \cdot \frac{1}{8} = \frac{39}{16} =$
$2\frac{7}{16}$ in.

b) Area of triangle: $A = \frac{1}{2}bh \rightarrow$

$\frac{1}{2}\left(2\frac{1}{4}\right)\left(\frac{15}{16}\right) = \frac{1}{2}\left(\frac{9}{4}\right)\left(\frac{15}{16}\right) = \frac{135}{128} =$

$1\frac{7}{128}$ in.^{2}

Area of business card: $A = 3\frac{1}{2} \cdot 2 =$

$\frac{7}{2} \cdot \frac{2}{1} = 7$ in.^{2}

Difference: $7 - 1\frac{7}{128} = 5\frac{121}{128}$ in.^{2}
There would be about 6 in.^{2} left for other information on the business card.

6) *Sample answer:* a) and b) Journalists and mathematicians would not provide meaningful results because they have already graduated from college. c) High school students would provide meaningful results since the majority of them will take college entrance exams.

7) Test market results: $\frac{74,925}{2,775,000} = 0.027$

2.7% of customers signed up for the service
Projected number of customers nationwide:
185,250,000 · 0.027 = 5,001,750
Since the projected number of customers exceed the minimum necessary to be profitable, the service is expected to be profitable if made available nationwide.

Unit 7: Architecture
Drawing Geometric Shapes (p. 53)
2)

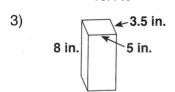

3)

8 in.   3.5 in.   5 in.

4) It is not possible to draw a cube with these dimensions because all of the dimensions of a cube must be the same.

5)

49 mm   22 mm

6) It is not possible to draw a triangle with these angle measures because the sum of the measures is greater than 180°.

Calculating Dimensions of Scale Models (p. 54)

2) $\frac{1 \text{ cm}}{2 \text{ m}} = \frac{x}{87 \text{ m}} \rightarrow \frac{(2 \text{ m})(x)}{2 \text{ m}} = \frac{(1 \text{ cm})(87 \text{ m})}{2 \text{ m}}$
$\rightarrow x = 43.5$ cm
$\frac{1 \text{ cm}}{2 \text{ m}} = \frac{x}{42 \text{ m}} \rightarrow \frac{(2 \text{ m})(x)}{2 \text{ m}} = \frac{(1 \text{ cm})(42 \text{ m})}{2 \text{ m}}$
$\rightarrow x = 21$ cm
The dimensions of the model are 43.5 cm by 21 cm.

3) $\frac{1 \text{ in.}}{4 \text{ yd}} = \frac{x}{112 \text{ yd}} \rightarrow \frac{(4 \text{ yd})(x)}{4 \text{ yd}} = \frac{(1 \text{ in.})(112 \text{ yd})}{4 \text{ yd}}$
$\rightarrow x = 28$ in.
$\frac{1 \text{ in.}}{4 \text{ yd}} = \frac{x}{372 \text{ yd}} \rightarrow \frac{(4 \text{ yd})(x)}{4 \text{ yd}} = \frac{(1 \text{ in.})(372 \text{ yd})}{4 \text{ yd}}$
$\rightarrow x = 93$ in.
The dimensions of the model are 28 in. by 93 in.

4) $\frac{1 \text{ m}}{0.5 \text{ in.}} = \frac{x}{2 \text{ in.}} \rightarrow \frac{(0.5 \text{ in.})(x)}{0.5 \text{ in.}} = \frac{(1 \text{ m})(2 \text{ in.})}{0.5 \text{ in.}}$
$\rightarrow x = 4$ m
$\frac{1 \text{ m}}{0.5 \text{ in.}} = \frac{x}{9 \text{ in.}} \rightarrow \frac{(0.5 \text{ in.})(x)}{0.5 \text{ in.}} = \frac{(1 \text{ m})(9 \text{ in.})}{0.5 \text{ in.}}$
$\rightarrow x = 18$ m
The dimensions of the model are 4 m by 18 m.

5) $\frac{1 \text{ cm}}{10 \text{ m}} = \frac{x}{98.5 \text{ m}} \rightarrow \frac{(10 \text{ m})(x)}{10 \text{ m}} = \frac{(1 \text{ cm})(98.5 \text{ m})}{10 \text{ m}}$
$\rightarrow x = 9.85$ cm
$\frac{1 \text{ cm}}{10 \text{ m}} = \frac{x}{135.2 \text{ m}} \rightarrow \frac{(10 \text{ m})(x)}{10 \text{ m}} = \frac{(1 \text{ cm})(135.2 \text{ m})}{10 \text{ m}}$
$\rightarrow x = 13.52$ cm
The dimensions of the model are 9.85 cm by 13.52 cm.

6) $\frac{1 \text{ ft}}{0.1 \text{ cm}} = \frac{x}{8.3 \text{ cm}} \rightarrow \frac{(0.1 \text{ cm})(x)}{0.1 \text{ cm}} = \frac{(1 \text{ ft})(8.3 \text{ cm})}{0.1 \text{ cm}}$
$\rightarrow x = 83$ ft
$\frac{1 \text{ ft}}{0.1 \text{ cm}} = \frac{x}{4.9 \text{ cm}} \rightarrow \frac{(0.1 \text{ cm})(x)}{0.1 \text{ cm}} = \frac{(1 \text{ ft})(4.9 \text{ cm})}{0.1 \text{ cm}}$
$\rightarrow x = 49$ ft
The dimensions of the model are 83 ft by 49 ft.

Complementary, Supplementary and Adjacent Angles (p. 55)
2) The angles are complementary.;
$m = 90° - 64°$ or 26°
3) The sum of the angle measures is 180°.;
$a = 180° - (35° + 82°)$ or 63°
4) The angles are supplementary.;
$b = 180° - 112°$ or 68°
5) The angles are complementary.;
$y = 90° - 53°$ or 37°
6) The sum of the angle measures is 180°.;
$d = 180° - (49° + 108°)$ or 23°

7) The angles are complementary, so the measure of the complement of an angle with a measure of 29° is 90° − 29° or 61°.

8) The angles are supplementary, so the measure of the supplement of an angle with a measure of 136° is 180° − 136° or 44°.

The Mathematics of Architecture (p. 56–62)

1)

2) Side length of base: $\left(\frac{3}{4}\right)$(756 ft) = 567 ft

   Height: $\left(\frac{3}{4}\right)$(481 ft) = 360.75 ft.

3)
   a) The length of the edge must be 719.1 feet because the sum of the length of any two sides of a triangle must be greater than the length of the third side. The sum of the two given sides of the triangle in #2 is 1,015.6. Therefore, the length of the third side could not be 1,019.1.

   b) Edge of pyramid: $\left(\frac{3}{4}\right)$(719.1 ft) = 539.325 ft

4)
   a) *Sample answer:* 1 cm = 100 ft or 1 in. = 100 ft

   b) *Sample answer:* For 1 cm = 100 ft:
      Side length of base:
      $$\frac{1 \text{ cm}}{100 \text{ ft}} = \frac{x}{567 \text{ ft}} \rightarrow \frac{(1 \text{ cm})(567 \text{ ft})}{100 \text{ ft}} = \frac{(100 \text{ ft})(x)}{100 \text{ ft}}$$
      $$\rightarrow 5.67 \text{ cm} = x$$
      Height:
      $$\frac{1 \text{ cm}}{100 \text{ ft}} = \frac{x}{360.75 \text{ ft}} \rightarrow \frac{(1 \text{ cm})(360.75 \text{ ft})}{100 \text{ ft}} = \frac{(100 \text{ ft})(x)}{100 \text{ ft}}$$
      $$\rightarrow 3.61 \text{ cm} = x$$
      For 1 in. = 100 ft: Side length of base is 5.67 in. and height is 3.61 in.

   c) Answers will vary.

5) My pyramid will be 360.75 feet tall. So it can have 360.75 ÷ 10 or 36 stories.

6) The company should not be concerned about the shape of the floor. The floors will be squares because the base of the pyramid is a square and the floors will all be parallel to the base.

7) The walls will be in the shape of a trapezoid because they will be perpendicular to the base but will not pass through the vertex of the pyramid.

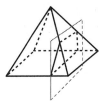

8) Lateral surface area of the pyramid:
   $(4)\left(\frac{1}{2}\right)$(567)(458.8) = 520,279.2 ft²
   I will need 520,279.2 square feet of glass for all four sides.

9) Because the obtuse angle of the rhombus forms a straight angle with an angle that has a measure of 60°, I know that the angles are supplementary. So the measure of *o* is 180° − 60° or 120°.

10)
   a) This design would require there to be triangular, rectangular, and trapezoidal shaped windows.

   b) The 35° angle and angle *x* are both adjacent to a right angle that is part of the rectangular shaped window. Together, the three angles form a straight angle so, *x* = 180° − (35° + 90°) or 55°. My officemate calculated the correct angle measure.

Unit 8: Nursing
Unit Conversions (p. 64)

2) 50 yd $\cdot \dfrac{3 \text{ ft}}{1 \text{ yd}} \cdot \dfrac{12 \text{ in.}}{1 \text{ ft}} \cdot \dfrac{2.54 \text{ cm}}{1 \text{ in.}} \cdot \dfrac{1 \text{ m}}{100 \text{ cm}}$
   = 45.72 in.

3) 75 lb $\cdot \dfrac{1 \text{ kg}}{2.2 \text{ lb}}$ = 34.09 kg

4) 180 kg $\cdot \dfrac{1,000 \text{ g}}{1 \text{ kg}} \cdot \dfrac{1 \text{ lb}}{453.6 \text{ g}} \cdot \dfrac{16 \text{ oz}}{1 \text{ lb.}}$
   = 6,349.21 oz

5) 300 c $\cdot \dfrac{1 \text{ qt}}{4 \text{ c}} \cdot \dfrac{1 \text{ L}}{1.06 \text{ qt}}$ = 70.75 L

6) 215 mL $\cdot \dfrac{0.034 \text{ fl oz}}{1 \text{ mL}}$ = 7.31 fl oz

7) 42 L $\cdot \dfrac{1.06 \text{ qt}}{1 \text{ L}} \cdot \dfrac{1 \text{ gal}}{4 \text{ qt}}$ = 11.13 gal

8) 2.5 mi $\cdot \dfrac{5,280 \text{ ft}}{1 \text{ mi}} \cdot \dfrac{12 \text{ in.}}{1 \text{ ft}} \cdot \dfrac{2.54 \text{ cm}}{1 \text{ in.}} \cdot$
   $\dfrac{1 \text{ m}}{100 \text{ cm}} \cdot \dfrac{1 \text{ km}}{1,000 \text{ m}}$ = 4.02 km

What Are the Chances? (p. 65)
2) Unlikely
3) Impossible
4) Likely
5) Certain
6) Unlikely
7) Equally likely to occur or not to occur
8) Extremely unlikely
9) Equally likely to occur or not to occur
10) Likely

Mean Absolute Deviation (p. 66)
2) Mean = 65; MAD = 24
3) Mean = 5.85; MAD = 2.21
4) Mean ≈ 168.1; MAD ≈ 70.9

The Mathematics of Nursing (p. 67–71)
1)
   a) $18 \text{ lb} \cdot \dfrac{1 \text{ kg}}{2.2 \text{ lb}} = 8.18 \text{ kg}$
     Taria weighs 8.18 kg.
   b) $8.18 \text{ kg} \cdot 15 \text{ mg/kg} = 122.7 \text{ mg}$
     Taria should receive 122.7 mg per dose.
   c) $\dfrac{160 \text{ mg}}{5 \text{ mL}} = \dfrac{122.7 \text{ mg}}{x \text{ mL}} \longrightarrow 160x = 613.5$
     $\longrightarrow x = 3.83$
     Taria should receive 3.83 mL of acetaminophen.

2) 65 lbs = 29.55 kg
   $29.55 \text{ kg} \cdot 15 \text{ mg/kg} = 443.25 \text{ mg}$
   $\dfrac{160 \text{ mg}}{5 \text{ mL}} = \dfrac{443.25 \text{ mg}}{x \text{ mL}} \longrightarrow 160x = 2{,}216.25$
   $\longrightarrow x = 13.85$
   Santino should receive 13.85 mL of acetaminophen.

3) The likelihood of any of these side effects is very small. Difficulty breathing is least likely at 0.2%. Only 1 out of 10 people experience a skin reaction. Even fewer people experience drowsiness. Nausea has the greatest likelihood of presenting, at 12%.

4)
   a) Because the probability of experiencing a skin reaction is 1 out of 10, I can randomly select a digit between 0 and 9 to represent the side effect. For example, a 0 could represent a patient with a skin reaction as a result of taking Medication A, and the digits 1 through 9 would represent patients who did not experience that side effect.
   b) A trial for this scenario would be to select a string of eight random digits.

   c) A success in a trial for this scenario is the occurrence of one or more 0's in a string of eight digits.
   d) *Sample answer:*
     57455724 – failure
     55939490 – success
     30173346 – success
     35061265 – success
     97618630 – success
     26080991 – success
     35011771 – success
     81103184 – success
     63314499 – failure
     17543471 – failure
     29341070 – success
     96696438 – failure
     55662510 – success
     76905816 – success
     09853085 – success
     88020301 – success
     08814693 – success
     34875593 – failure
     63459473 – failure
     31270522 – success
   e. $\dfrac{14}{20} = 70\%$; The probability that at least 1 of the 8 patients Dody calls will have experienced a skin reaction is 70%.

5) *Sample answer:* It appears that men stay 6–8 days while women only stay 4–7 days.
6) *Sample answer:* It appears that the men have a greater variability.
7) Mean ≈ 7.87; MAD ≈ 3.54
8) Mean ≈ 8.67; MAD ≈ 3.60
9) *Sample answer:* I was correct in thinking that the men had longer hospital stays; their mean is about 1 day longer than the women's mean. However, the MADs for the men and women are very close, indicating that they have about the same variability.
10) Lorenzo should tell the family that the average stay is between 7–8 days for women and 8–9 days for men. He should explain, though, that this varies by about 3–4 days for both men and women.

Unit 9: Accounting
Fractions (p. 73)

2) $\frac{1}{6} \cdot 720 = \$120$

3) $\frac{1}{6} \cdot \frac{1}{4} \cdot \frac{822,000}{1} = \frac{822,000}{24} = \$34,250$

4) $\frac{135}{855} = \frac{27}{171} = \frac{3}{19}$

5) Fraction of account balance represented by $642:

$1 - \frac{17}{20} = \frac{3}{20} \longrightarrow \frac{3}{20} = \frac{642}{x} \longrightarrow$

$3x = 12,840 \longrightarrow x = 4,280$

The woman's account had $4,280 before the withdrawal.

6) $\frac{6}{25} \div \frac{16}{15} = \frac{\cancel{6}^{3}}{\cancel{25}_{5}} \cdot \frac{\cancel{15}^{3}}{\cancel{16}_{8}} = \frac{9}{40}$

7) $\frac{4}{5} \div \frac{8}{15} - \frac{1}{2} \cdot \frac{3}{4} = \frac{\cancel{4}^{1}}{\cancel{5}_{1}} \cdot \frac{\cancel{15}^{3}}{\cancel{8}_{2}} - \frac{1}{2} \cdot \frac{3}{4}$

$= \frac{3}{2} - \frac{3}{8} = \frac{12}{8} - \frac{3}{8} = \frac{9}{8} = 1\frac{1}{8}$

8) $\frac{510}{1800} = \frac{51}{180} = \frac{17}{60}$; The boy would spend $\frac{17}{60}$ of his savings on the new bicycle.

Percents (p. 74)

2) $349.99 \cdot 1.07 = 374.4893$; The total cost of the item after tax is $374.49.

3) 30% of 40%: $0.3 \cdot 0.4 = 0.12$;
40% + 12% = 52%; 52% goes to payroll.

4) Amount of decrease: 28% − 25% = 3%;

Percent decrease: $\frac{0.03}{0.28} \approx 0.1071$

The marketing department experienced a decrease in funding of approximately 10.7%.

5) $\frac{x}{100} = \frac{208}{640} \longrightarrow 640x = 20,800 \longrightarrow$

$x = \frac{20,800}{640} = 32.5\%$

6) $0.35 \cdot 0.72 \cdot 380 = 95.76$

7) Amount of taxes:
$72,546.93 - 51,798.51 = 20,748.42$;

$\frac{20,748.42}{72,546.93} \approx 0.2860$

The man paid approximately 28.6% in taxes.

8) $\frac{85}{100} = \frac{27,540}{x} \longrightarrow 85x = 2,754,000 \longrightarrow$

$x = \frac{2,754,000}{85} = 32,400$

$32,400

Linear Equations and Inequalities (p. 75)

2) $A = 350 + 40m$

3) $12(x + 11) > 8 \longrightarrow 12x + 132 > 8 \longrightarrow$

$12x > -124 \longrightarrow x > -\frac{\cancel{124}^{31}}{\cancel{12}_{3}} \longrightarrow$

$x > -\frac{31}{3}$ or $x > -10\frac{1}{3}$

4) $400 + 0.08m \geq 1,000$

5) $15(x - 3) = 120$

6) $\frac{\cancel{4}}{\cancel{3}} \cdot \frac{\cancel{3}}{\cancel{4}}(x + 22) = \frac{1}{2} \cdot \frac{\cancel{4}^{2}}{3} \longrightarrow x + 22 = \frac{2}{3}$

$\longrightarrow x = \frac{2}{3} - \frac{66}{3} \longrightarrow x = -\frac{64}{3}$ or $x = -21\frac{1}{3}$

The Mathematics of Accounting (p. 76–80)

1)
a) Amount of increase this year: 15% of 9.6%; $0.15 \cdot 0.096 = 0.0144 = 1.44\%$;
9.6% + 1.44% = 11.04%;
R&D is allocated 11.04% of the total budget this year.

b) Let x represent the dollar amount of the company's total budget last year;
R&D budget last year: $0.096x$;
R&D budget this year:
$0.1104(1.25x) = 0.138x$
Increase in R&D budget:
$0.138x - 0.096x = 0.042x$
The gain experienced by R&D this year is equal to 4.2% of the company's total budget last year.
Percent increase in amount allocated to R&D:
$\frac{0.042}{0.096} = 0.4375 = 43.75\%$
There is an increase of 43.75% in the dollar amount allocated to R&D this year.

2) Total salary paid: $3 \cdot 4,622.55 = 13,867.65$;
Total benefits paid: $3 \cdot 478.52 = 1,435.56$;
Total paid: $13,867.65 + 1,435.56 + 14,562.83 + 7,551.24 + 3,090.92 = 40,508.20$
To break even, the business must take in as much as is paid out. Therefore, the business must generate $40,508.20 this month to break even.

3) Quality Control: 7,500 per month
   Marketing: $7{,}500 + 11{,}000 = 18{,}500$ per month
   Payroll: $4 \cdot 18{,}500 = 74{,}000$ per month
   $(7{,}500 + 18{,}500 + 74{,}000)m = 500{,}000$
   $\longrightarrow 100{,}000m = 500{,}000 \longrightarrow m = 5$
   The three departments can operate for 5 months before the budget is depleted.

4) Personal income tax: $0.0307 \cdot 58{,}427.90 = 1{,}793.73653 \longrightarrow \$1{,}793.74$
   Inheritance tax: $0.045 \cdot 25{,}000 = 1{,}125 \longrightarrow \$1{,}125.00$
   Total tax paid: $1{,}793.74 + 1{,}125 = 2{,}918.74$
   The client must pay \$2,918.74 in state taxes.

5) AlgebraTech still owns $\frac{3}{5}$ of the company after TrigCorp's investment.
   $\frac{3}{5} \div 4 = \frac{3}{5} \cdot \frac{1}{4} = \frac{3}{20} = 0.15 = 15\%$
   Each founder owns 15% of the company after TrigCorp's investment.

6) Let x represent the company's net income at the beginning of the study.
   After year 1: $x + 0.3x = 1.3x$
   After year 2: $1.3x + 0.4(1.3x) = 1.3x + 0.52x = 1.82x$
   After year 3: $1.82x - 0.15(1.82x) = 1.82x - 0.273x = 1.547x$
   After year 4: $1.547x + 0.25(1.547x) = 1.547x + 0.38675x = 1.93375x$
   After year 5: $1.93375x - 0.1(1.93375x) = 1.93375x - 0.193375x = 1.740375x$
   There was an increase of approximately 74.04% in net income since the study began.

7) Price without sales tax: $15{,}506.21 \div 1.06 = 14{,}628.50 \longrightarrow \$14{,}628.50$
   Amount of sales tax:
   $15{,}506.21 - 14{,}628.50 = 877.71$
   The organization overpaid by \$877.71 due to being charged sales tax on the furniture.

8)
   a) Total cost to manufacture 1,000 items of new product: $720 + 1{,}000(6.84) = 720 + 6{,}840 = 7{,}560$
      $\frac{7{,}560}{94{,}500} = 0.08 = 8\%$
      To manufacture 1,000 items of the new product, 8% of the available budget must be used.

   b) Cost to manufacture 1,000 items of new product: \$7,560
      Total amount of revenue required to proceed: $\$7{,}560 \cdot 2 = \$15{,}120$
      Unit price per item:
      $15{,}120 \div 1{,}000 = 15.12 = \$15.12$